DE GRUYTER

JERRY ANGRAVE

THE JOURNEY MAPPING PLAYBOOK

A practical guide to preparing, facilitating and unlocking the value of customer journey mapping

DE
G

Dedication

To Caroline, Charlie and Freya

DOWNLOAD

Worksheets marked with this
icon can be downloaded here:

▷ **www.degruyter.com/books/9783110641110**

TABLE OF CONTENTS

FOREWORD

I always knew that Customer Experience was very important, but I didn't realise it was a science – "and behind that science is a heart".

This quote, delivered to me by the senior leader of a bank, has stuck with me ever since. Even as someone who has been involved from the very beginning with the profession that Customer Experience [CX] has become, I did not realise until the moment I heard this amazing lady say it, that Customer Experience *is* a science.

Although the science is a simple one in principle, it is underpinned by a number of competencies. I say simple "in principle" because the competencies are not difficult to understand conceptually. However, turning the concept into practical, demonstrable action is a different thing altogether.

One of the most important competencies that defines the science is the understanding and managing of the customer journey. Customer journey mapping has become a "business phenomenon" over the last few years. As I always say, many organisations have been mapping customer journeys until they are "coming out of their ears" – metaphorically speaking, obviously!

However, despite the customer journey becoming a well-known "tool", regrettably, many still do not understand exactly what a customer journey map *should* visualise and, even more importantly, *what* to do with it! I am therefore delighted that Jerry is sharing his considerable knowledge and expertise on the what, why and how of customer journey mapping with the world.

Jerry epitomises *both* the science of Customer Experience *and* the heart. In this book, he brilliantly describes how to go about creating a customer journey map so it can be effectively used to drive demonstrable change. With wonderful simplicity and clarity, he describes how to set things up for success and address the "So what?" that too many organisations miss altogether.

This book should and will become an essential read for any CX practitioner – whether they are new to the profession or not. Enjoy the read!

IAN GOLDING
Global Customer Experience Specialist
Certified Customer Experience Professional

INTRODUCTION

A warm welcome and a big "Thank you" for choosing this book to guide your own journey of JOURNEY MAPPING.

I f there is one element of Customer Experience guaranteed to bring people together, raise challenging questions and showcase how companies can benefit from being more customer-centric, it's journey mapping. I've always said, if you do nothing else in the name of Customer Experience, map a customer journey and see where it takes you.

Why? Because if we want to get the most out of any relationship we must have → EMPATHY – the ability to understand and share what it's really like for others. Without empathy we simply impose our own beliefs and expect customers to comply with our own processes.

Habit number five of Steven Covey's *The 7 Habits of Highly Successful People*[1] advised, "Seek first to understand then be understood". Whether we're talking about customers or internal stakeholders – and this book is about both – it's advice that has stuck with me for years and is at the bedrock of customer journey mapping.

So, first, what do we mean by "journey mapping"? It's a tool used by Customer Experience professionals around the world as a method of documenting what it's really like to be a customer and to prioritise what should be done about that experience.

It's not a process map. It's not just about sticky notes on the wall. It's about writing the narrative of what your customers do, think and feel when they do business with you in a way that helps you drive meaningful change.

If you have customers, you are already giving them a customer experience. We can improve those experiences simply by making our existing processes better. Or, we can be truly customer-centric by first designing those processes around how we fit into our customers' lives. Journey mapping shows us how. Importantly though, it also shows great experiences that already exist and that should be celebrated more and protected.

Journey mapping is many people's favourite part of Customer Experience, including me. It's engaging, it's fun and it can be provocative.

Journey mapping is an experience in itself. In the same way that you want your customers to come back, buy more and share the right stories with others, your workshops will be such that attendees want to come back for another session, they become fully engaged with your programme and they act as advocates for the CX work you are doing.

That's what this *Playbook* is all about. How do you plan, facilitate and then demonstrate the value of journey

→ EMPATHY
The ability to understand and share the feelings of another.

1 UNDERSTAND, THEN BE UNDERSTOOD
Covey, S. R., *The 7 Habits of Highly Successful People*, Simon & Schuster, UK, 2004.

mapping by providing a compelling argument to make changes? The central core of this book is the workshop. I've set out a plan you can follow, an agenda and tips for keeping everything on track. However, just as importantly, either side of that we'll spend time first looking at how to prepare for those workshops so they are strategically supportive and highly effective when you run them. We'll then explore what you do with the output of the workshop to ensure you and your business get the most out of them.

By all means, go straight to the journey map template, but it will be at its most effective when it's put in the right context.

We'll take you through not just the how-to of journey mapping in a way that you can then run your own sessions but we'll also see where it fits in the wider context of Customer Experience. Journey mapping cannot be done in a vacuum, as a one-off workshop. It's a great place to start but it must also be part of, and contribute to, the Customer Experience programme, business strategy and overall culture of an organisation.

» Preparation, I have often said, is rightly two-thirds of any venture. «
AMELIA EARHART

USE JOURNEY MAPPING TO STRESS-TEST THE REAL CULTURE

For example, I once ran a series of journey mapping workshops for a top-25 accountancy firm. We were using their very plush training room overlooking the heart of London's financial district. There was good attendance with colleagues from all the different parts of the business including a handful of senior partners.

We talked about their values, which were pretty much exactly the same as many other professional services firms; global expertise, communication, trust, value and so on. Very inward-looking. So with one of their slides over my shoulder proudly proclaiming that "We put clients at the heart of everything we do", I suggested that it was worth finding time in day-to-day conversations or annual reviews to understand what those values mean to clients on a daily basis. What's it like to be the CEO, Finance Director or Head of Accounts who is directly or indirectly on the receiving end of what the accountancy firm does?

In one of the sessions, a senior partner piped up at this point and through his scowl said, "Jerry, the only way I'm going to allow anyone to talk to clients about that sort of stuff is if I can bill the client for the time it takes."

Mouths dropped open and it all went quiet. Complacency was hard at work for this "leader". He assured me that things were okay. They have happy clients (yes, their satisfaction scores were okay), they were making money (of course) and their people were happy (apparently). So why change anything or spend any more money than they had to? I pointed out that they'd make more money, have prouder colleagues and higher satisfaction scores than their competitors if they took more notice of clients and how the firm contributed to the clients' success. He didn't buy it.

Later that day when we were identifying the customer measures they had in place or they needed, the same senior partner scored another sizzler. He took a sticky note, found a red marker pen and wrote in big capital letters, "CASH IS KING". He then left the room, explaining that cash is the only thing that matters to a business and that he had important business to attend to.

The question is:
Is cash the king?

The reason I share this anecdote is because a journey mapping session is not just about writing down ideas and getting them on the wall. We'll look at the benefits of customer journey mapping later, but it can lead to some profound outcomes. After some reflection on how committed it was, this accountancy firm did revisit its values and asked clients for their input. However, at least one person I know left the organisation a few weeks afterwards, citing a toxic culture and leadership behaviours that were still not consistent with the firm's values.

If you have such an eventful or provocative workshop it is probably no bad thing. Those conversations need to be had and if it's your session that is the catalyst for stress-testing how customer-centric the business is, then that should be seen as a feather in your cap.

So my aim with this *Playbook* is to give you a guide so you can plan, host and get the most value from your own journey mapping work. It will provide food for thought, templates and tips about how to make your own journey mapping strategic, effective and influential.

Too often, the impact of journey mapping is limited; according to a 2019 report by *Gartner*[1], 82% of companies had mapped customer journeys yet only 47% are using them effectively. That's a lot of wasted effort and no doubt as a consequence, a lot of disillusioned and cynical stakeholders.

This *Playbook* is written in a way to help ensure you are creating and using journey mapping sessions effectively and that your stakeholders see the benefits and support you in doing more.

The methodology I cover can be used in a wide variety of scenarios and in both consumer and business-to-business markets. Where I use the term "customer", this could equally be a client, patient, member, passenger, student, citizen, guest or visitor.

The suggestions and recommendations are based on my own time as an in-house CX practitioner in the corporate world. Since 2012 I have run my own Customer Experience consulting and coaching company. What you have in this *Playbook* is a distillation of what I've seen work and what, to put it politely, didn't go according to plan at all.

In that time I've had the pleasure of running countless workshops all over Europe and the Middle East and with companies in all types of sectors. I've mapped journeys with three people in the room and with 43. The context and methodology, however, stay the same.

In my time as a CX professional both in-house and as a consultant I've seen many companies finding it easy

1 REPORT BY GARTNER
Pannetta, K., *How to Create an Effective Customer Journey Map*, Gartner, 10 June 2019.

IF YOU DO NOTHING ELSE IN THE NAME OF CUSTOMER EXPERIENCE, ESPECIALLY IN A POST COVID-19 WORLD, HAVE A GO AT JOURNEY MAPPING AND SEE WHERE IT TAKES YOU. YOUR BOSS AND CUSTOMERS WILL THANK YOU FOR IT.

to say, "We put customers at the heart of everything we do". Without concrete actions backed up by facts and credible evidence, however, belief and passion will quickly fade back to the day job, a myopic focus on operational metrics and the P&L.

I am no expert or self-proclaimed guru, far from it. But I have run many, many journey mapping sessions and have seen what makes them successful and what can undermine them. It's a privilege to share those lessons in this *Playbook*.

It must be said, there is no one way to map customer journeys. Every CX professional and organisation will do it slightly differently. I hope that in time you develop your own methodology. In the meantime, the structure and principles set out here will get you started and well on the way.

The approach to journey mapping I've outlined is deliberately low tech. Mostly, zero tech. Software platforms and visualisation tools can be beneficial but the focus here is on getting the core principles of journey mapping right. The outputs can then be enhanced by technology if it suits your needs but I did not want the effectiveness of the process to be diluted by having a goal of making everything digital.

WHO IS THE BOOK FOR?

The people who will get the most from this book are those in the early stages of their own journey, building a rewarding career in Customer Experience.

→ CX, and journey mapping itself, can be a daunting thing. It's not an exact science because at its heart it's a way of thinking, a mindset. We know the commercial benefits it can deliver yet it doesn't fit neatly into a business case methodology. I'll therefore share frameworks and tips that will allow you to run your own workshops and become known in your company as the go-to Customer Experience person.

If you are a seasoned Customer Experience practitioner, it is very likely that you'll have your own approach, nurtured over the years. I hope you discover something of value here but I don't want to patronise anyone who's been on the front line of a journey mapping programme and learned by experience.

On the other hand, if you are a "Customer Experience consultant" the book should have nothing new for you. If you are advising others on the subject of Customer Experience and CX programmes with any credibility you should, at the very least, know your way around journey mapping. The workshop methodology is one thing but that alone is not journey mapping. You will have led your own sessions as an in-house practitioner yourself and learned by experience how you prefer to do things. You'll have the battle scars from going toe-to-toe with sceptical line managers to make changes. If you are a CX consultant but journey mapping is still new to you, well, I'll leave it there.

HOW IS THE BOOK STRUCTURED?

The easiest way to think about this book is as a journey in its own right, with you as its persona. In its broadest terms, we have three stages to take you through, the "Before, During and After" (›see Figure 1). Journey mapping is all about organising your thinking and it's no different here. For our purposes, we'll therefore focus on thorough planning (Chapter II), effective facilitation (Chapter III) and acting on the findings (Chapter IV).

It's a real pleasure to share my thoughts on journey mapping with you. That you are interested in journey mapping is a strong indicator of your passion as a CX

→ CX
Customer Experience

FIGURE 1

Three stage journey: In this book we'll explore each stage in our own journey of journey mapping.

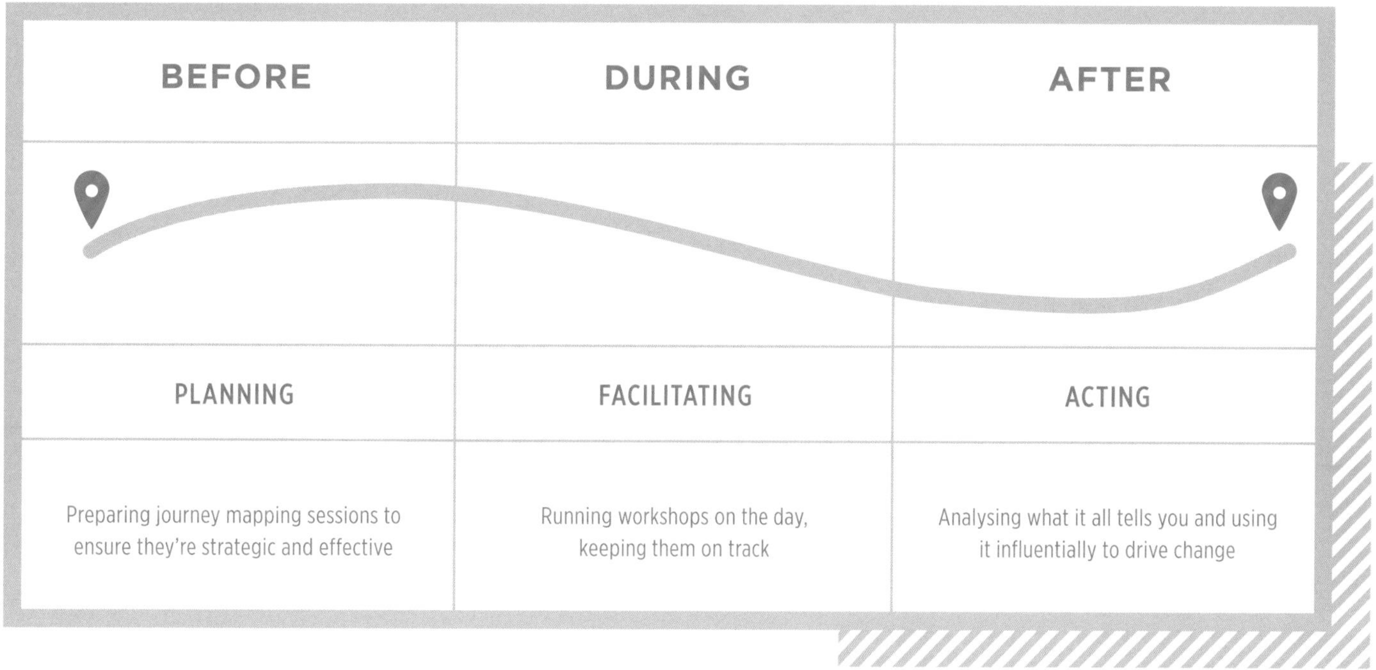

BEFORE	DURING	AFTER
PLANNING	FACILITATING	ACTING
Preparing journey mapping sessions to ensure they're strategic and effective	Running workshops on the day, keeping them on track	Analysing what it all tells you and using it influentially to drive change

professional and of your genuine desire to help your organisation improve.

The beauty of journey mapping is that it goes way beyond a day-long workshop with sticky notes. It pokes a stick at the organisational culture to understand why things are as they are and how it makes employees feel. And it asks searching questions of the strategy if there appears to be a lack of clarity about exactly how good the business is trying to be.

I'll explore these factors in the book and would encourage you, as you build and run your own journey mapping programme, to embrace those conversations about the wider issues. If something is having an effect on the Customer or Employee Experience, then we need to know that so we can do something about it. Look for those cans of worms, open them and dive right in!

A QUICK WORD ABOUT COVID-19

In the latter stages of writing this book the world went into lockdown as it responded to Covid-19. To ignore its presence and impact on journey mapping would be to ignore a huge elephant in the room.

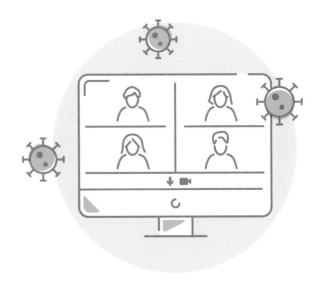

The new reality of remote working
in a post-Covid world

One of the biggest advantages of journey mapping is the physical act of bringing people together in the same room. They huddle in groups, working shoulder to shoulder around the journey maps they are creating. To state the obvious, it's likely to be a while before we can get back to those days.

In the meantime though, the underlying principles of finding the most value from journey mapping still apply. It is possible to run an effective journey mapping workshop remotely and we'll look at how to do that and how things might be different in Chapter III.

ONE LAST THOUGHT BEFORE WE BEGIN

We must be realistic. Journey mapping on its own will not unlock the full potential and commercial benefits of an organisation that obsesses about its customers. It will take a clear and shared vision of how the organisation wants to make its customers feel. It will take a leadership team that's fully committed to that vision and works in harmony across functions. Fundamentally, it will take a belief that better experiences do lead to better business and an acceptance that the organisation must earn the right to customer-led growth.

However, journey mapping will provide the direction, the compass by which that vision can be reached. Without taking such an empathetic, customer perspective it's much harder to know where the tactical priorities lie, what the implications for strategic decision-making are and how the culture needs to change.

So, let's get started and go on this incredible journey together.   «

PART 1

WORKSHOP PREPARATION

CHAP

SETTING THE SCENE

We could jump in and go straight to the workshop. However, to be truly effective, customer journey mapping must not be done in a vacuum. It has to support the wider CX programme and be focused on what's important for the business as well as for customers. In this first chapter we therefore explore the wider context in which journey mapping sits.

JOURNEY MAPPING

THE JOURNEY MAP IS A VISUAL REPRESENTATION OF WHAT IT'S REALLY LIKE TO BE ONE OF YOUR CUSTOMERS, GIVING CLARITY AND DIRECTION IN TERMS OF WHAT TO DO ABOUT THAT EXPERIENCE.

If we start with the end, picturing what successful journey mapping might look like, we know what we're aiming for.

So, you're about to start your journey mapping workshop. The room's all set, everyone (well, most of them) eager to get started. You're hoping, after all the conversations you've had with the leadership team, that the Board will be impressed with the outcome of what you're about to do.

You take a deep breath and clear your head of everything apart from your three key messages about what you're doing, why it's important and what happens next. And then, harnessing your passion, energy and credibility, you give your colleagues a warm welcome and get the workshop under way.

During the day, they help you uncover what it's really like to be a customer. They become immersed in their personas and see their organisation from a different perspective. They meet colleagues they've never heard of but who are equally as important in delivering the right Customer Experience.

The workshop participants have all sorts of thoughts about what can be done better and how important this sort of exercise is. It might be the first time anyone has taken this perspective. They talk about deep-rooted issues that have an impact on CX and appreciate the chance to raise them again. Those who were sceptical initially are now fully engaged. At the end of the workshop they won't stop discussing ideas and issues.

The participants leave full of ideas and positivity. They tell everyone the next day what it was like and become your ambassadors as they help spread the good word about what you're doing.

And then you use what you've just done to convince your boss and the leadership that some things should be celebrated more and protected; others should be done differently. You persuade them that being more customer-centric won't happen just because there's a new vision statement. You earn your credibility and become the "go-to" person for anything to do with Customer Experience.

For your audience, they've just had a "journey". They are your "customers". To ensure we get the most out of it and they help recruit others for your next sessions you can treat it as such. During the various stages of the workshop, from the invitation to the day itself and the follow-up thank you message, you're asking: what did they get out of it, what was going through their head and how did you make them feel?

You reflect on what you'll do differently next time and why. How do you know how well you did and just what did they think? And, crucially, what do you do next?

That journey mapping workshop is central to this book and, more importantly, Customer Experience as a whole. If we just focus on the workshop itself, though, we'll miss the point.

However, it will fail if it's not planned properly, if it's not put in the right context or if it doesn't lead to a strengthening of your overall business performance. You can have a great day with sticky notes but if it's not strategically aligned it'll remain just that, a great day with sticky notes. Your stakeholders will quickly lose interest and everyone will go back to their silo and process-led day job.

TIP

Think of the people attending your workshop as your 'customers'. You want them to have an intentional experience they want to repeat and tell others about.

FUNCTION, EASE AND EMOTION

The *functional* aspect is binary; did it work or not? Was it as expected and was it reliable and consistent? Did it help me achieve what I wanted to achieve?

The second element is self-explanatory; how *easy* was it? What hurdles did you make me jump through to get to the functional benefit? How much effort did it take on my part?

The *emotional* component can be the combination of the first two. It can also be simply about how, for whatever reason, you make your customers feel. It's important because there's much research to show how emotions have a disproportionately large impact on buyer behaviour ...

DEFINITIONS

We therefore begin our journey of journey mapping by being clear about our definitions. To secure and maintain buy-in to what you're doing it's essential that you give a single, consistent and credible version of what journey mapping is all about.

We'll explode some myths and explain why, despite seeming obvious, having a greater understanding of customers is at the core of any organisation wanting to succeed by being more customer-focused.

The Customer Experience

The Customer Experience is the totality of what the customer has experienced for themselves, whether it's their own experience and/or based on what they've heard from others.

I'm indebted to Bruce Temkin (the "Godfather of CX", who heads up the XM Institute™ at Qualtrics®) for his very clear approach to what makes up the Customer Experience that any of us has. It is essentially rooted in three dimensions: FUNCTION, EASE and EMOTION.

So *the* Customer Experience is essentially what the customers remember about you, think of you and how that then determines their choices and behaviour in the future based on whether they had the outcome they were looking for, whether you made it easy for them and how you made them feel. Added to that is what they see and hear from others and what they believe to be true about you.

A bank can make it easy to open a current account. In-branch, the experience might be exceptional. However, that customer may also have just heard the bank has also been fined millions of pounds for misselling insurance products. Will they buy again?

An airport can spend a fortune on its built environment to make everything quick and easy. Yet it can all be undone because a friend is recounting a story on Facebook about how an overzealous security official barked orders at people who were already anxious.

An organisation's brand is not what the strapline says, it's what customers say to each other about it. The customer experience is the culmination of everything someone sees, hears and experiences first hand.

Your organisation's brand is not the logo or smart strapline; think of it as what your customers tell each other it is

Customer Experience

Where "*The* Customer Experience" is about what customers remember and how it affects their behaviour, "Customer Experience" in its purest form is more about our way of thinking, a business strategy and a philosophy. It's about the management of the business and how we orchestrate and operationalise all the component parts to ensure "The Customer Experience" is the right one.

Until it's just the way we do business, it's likely to be fronted by a CX team who will nurture the corporate mindset so that it becomes more customer-centric. They will show the reality of how things are today and how they should be tomorrow. The team will engage and involve employees and it will set a CX strategy and vision everyone gets behind. It will listen, measure, understand and then act on feedback. And, Customer Experience will be the discipline under whose wing journey mapping is found.

Customer-centricity

It's easy to say we're customer-centric but a genuine mindset appreciates how better experiences for customers means better commercial outcomes. Customer-centricity will have a clear purpose, driven by an understanding of how it contributes to its customers' lives. And it may mean being prepared to take less profit per customer but in the knowledge that "the Customer Experience" will attract far more customers.

It's not a fluffy side of Marketing or a corporate flavour of the month. Being customer-centric is something on which your commercial fortune rests.

Customer Journey

The customer journey is a documentation of what your customer does (or wants to do), thinks and feels before, during and after they interact with you. The journey is made up of several steps, each of which will see them carrying out tasks, having unanswered questions and feeling different emotions.

The customer journey is not about your process maps. Their journey may start well before any contact with you and may carry on well beyond their last interaction with you. The customer will go on to tell others what you're like and reflect on how it was last time to determine whether they'll do it again next time.

TIP
Customer Service is about what we do to, with or on behalf of our customers. Customer Experience is about how we make them feel when they think of us.

Customer Service

Primarily, customer service is what we set out to do for, to, with or on behalf of our customers. It's how we serve them, how we respond to them, how we connect with them. The Customer Experience is then what it feels like to be on the receiving end of that customer service.

For example, a rail operator whose brand claims "We're here to get you there", might encourage people to ask questions via its social media account, which is staffed from 8am to 8pm. A tick in the box for customer service. However, what happens to a passenger at 9pm who's confused about whether their train is running or not? A wall of silence is the Customer Experience they'll remember.

Empathy

The dictionary definition is "the ability to understand and share the feelings of others." Whether intentionally or not we evoke emotions (or apathy) in our customers. It's our job to understand not just the emotions but what's driving those emotions. And that's where it gets complicated, because to do that we need to know what their expectations, motivations, hopes, fears and wants were to start with.

Surveys and spreadsheets full of metrics will give us helpful data to point us in the right general direction, but having real empathy will pinpoint where we need to be. That's where journey mapping comes in. The better we are at that understanding and then acting on the insight, the greater the chances of being different and better than our competition.

Empathy on its own is not enough – companies must act. When we talk about companies, organisations or businesses, what we mean is people – some on the front line, some in the Board Room and others providing vital support. Giving them an empathetic customer perspective is a compelling way to bring them together.

EXPLODING A FEW MYTHS

I like to think I live in the real world but the noise around CX in recent years has been deafening. Much of it is well placed but in some cases it has been completely hijacked or misunderstood. Here are just a few of the most common myths about Customer Experience. It's good to be prepared to push back if you're presented with them.

As we've just discussed, **Customer Experience is not a new version of Customer Service.** It's very different and needs to be handled as such.

CX is not new. Companies do not choose whether or not to "do" CX. If they have customers then they are already giving experiences. The challenge is, is the experience the right one?

Customer Experience does not "own" the customer. Too often those with "Customer Experience" in their job title get handed responsibility for being a pseudo customer-contact centre, for answering customer handling complaints and reporting on regulatory compliance.

Customer Experience is not a function. True, many companies do have Customer Experience teams, indeed I've led a few in my time. But they are there in the hope that one day they'll do themselves out of a job when everything they stand for becomes just the way the entire organisation goes about its business.

Having a poster on the wall saying "We put customers at the heart of everything we do" does not automatically make you customer-centric. **The right behaviours, attitudes, decision making and actions in line with your CX vision do.**

Customer journey mapping will not solve everything. I will emphasise again that journey mapping is just the beginning, not the endgame. Just because a company maps customer journeys does make it benefit from being more customer-centric. That's like reading a fitness magazine and thinking it'll turn us into lean athletes overnight.

Customer Experience is not there purely to increase the scores. That can be done any number of ways and if that's the focus the experience will suffer. More, CX is about creating the right experiences first, so the numbers take care of themselves.

DEBUNKING
A few myths about Customer Experience

It's important to be clear about these things because along the way, especially as you head into your planning, you'll need to overcome objections as to why your work should be a priority for your stakeholders.

BENEFITS

You may have read about journey mapping, you may have already been involved in a workshop, but now you're looking to host your own. Exciting times, but you can't do it effectively on your own.

You'll need others to help you. They in turn will want to know why they should bother. What's in it for them and for the business as a whole? Why should they take time out to attend or release anyone in their team to join you?

You're going to need to convince the powers that be that you are not just running "another" training workshop or elaborate away day. You'll need to cite clear benefits but thankfully there are many to choose from. › Table 1 shows just 11 to start with.

JUST BECAUSE A COMPANY MAPS ITS CUSTOMERS' JOURNEYS WILL NOT MAKE IT CUSTOMER-CENTRIC. THAT'S LIKE READING A FITNESS MAGAZINE AND THINKING IT'LL TURN US INTO LEAN ATHLETES.

TABLE 1
Benefits of journey mapping

〜〜〜〜〜〜〜〜〜〜〜〜〜〜〜〜〜〜〜

1

A MUCH-NEEDED REALITY CHECK

It finds a starting point, an honest and objective reality check of where the business is today in terms of its customers

2

SHOWS WHAT WE HAVE TO DO

The core benefit; highlighting what actions to take based on real customer needs, hopes, expectations and emotions. If your brand positioning is all about making things easy, you can showcase the actions that will have the biggest impact in making a customer's interaction with you even easier

3

CHANGES THE MINDSET TO BE MORE CUSTOMER-ORIENTED

The work immerses the team in the world of a customer in a way that they have not previously experienced. It shows how they can and should look at their organisation differently on an ongoing basis in future. It forces them to step back from the day job and gets people talking about customers more

4

CREATE AND SHARE STORIES

Every customer-centric business needs to be telling stories to illustrate why it's important to change or protect things, even stories about your journey mapping session – the word will get around about how enjoyable and useful it was

5

CREATES A FOCUS

Actions and the allocation of resources are done with confidence because they're based on clear evidence about how they directly support the CX vision and overall business goals

6

EDUCATIONAL

You can pretty much guarantee that attendees will learn something new about their own organisation, how it works and makes its money and about the people who work there

7

BRINGS PEOPLE FROM ACROSS THE BUSINESS TOGETHER

Employees from cross-functional divisions forge new relationships, sharing their own challenges and successes, seeing how they fit in to the overall picture

TIP

The benefits of journey mapping go way beyond finding things to fix.

DONE EFFECTIVELY, THE RIPPLE-EFFECT OF JOURNEY MAPPING CREATES BENEFITS BEYOND YOUR WORKSHOP

8

SUPPORTS EMPLOYEE ENGAGEMENT OBJECTIVES

Make sure employees recognise this as another opportunity to voice their opinions about how things can be improved for them and their customers

9

STRENGTHENS OVERALL CUSTOMER EXPERIENCE PROGRAMME

You will know if you're missing the clarity of a CX vision and the guidance of a robust governance forum. You'll know exactly how you might innovate and what customer metrics you should be tracking. And, how you can communicate better and bring it all to life for colleagues everywhere

10

VERSATILE TOOL

The methodology is easily repeated for different personas on different journeys. The personas can be different customer types but can also be employees, partners and stakeholders.

Over time you will build a programme of journeys to map; some will be at a high level, some micro journeys.

11

HELPS MAKE LEADERS ACCOUNTABLE

Armed with your insights about the reality of today's experience and what it will take to improve, you can hold the leadership team to account and use this to question their commitment to the vision and values of the organisation

WHEN THE PENNY DROPPED

I once facilitated a series of journey mapping workshops for a global membership organisation. They represented practitioners in their field of expertise, held events, training and curated a highly-respected professional qualification. They had many moving parts in the company.

Mid-way through a morning session one of the attendees stood up. As she waved her arms around and called for everyone's attention, I feared I might be about to get thrown out. Thankfully, she wanted to make the point that this was the first time every part of the organisation involved in this particular journey had come together at the same time in the same room.

It was a key moment of realisation for everyone and a brilliant anecdote to play back to the leadership team later.

"NOTHING'S EVER BEEN DONE"

HR may not be the first port of call for a customer journey mapping session but the link between employees and customers is unbreakable. A large energy retailer asked me and a couple of colleagues to get to the bottom of why they had so many complaints. To be clear, from the outset the leadership team made it plain that the problem was not their people. After all, the employee engagement survey was scoring an average nine out of ten.

I ran journey mapping workshops to get a grip on the Customer Experience and to hear the teams' views. It quickly transpired that there were many known issues contributing to the number of complaints.

Among them was that agents didn't have access to the tools or information that would help them reconcile queries on statements. There was no directory of who to ask about certain tricky questions. The contact centre was open from 8.30am to 5.30pm yet many small business owners do their administration at either end of the day. Customers who wanted to be reconnected were perplexed when they had to be put through to the debt recovery team. And if a small business owner rang from their home, the telephony system recognised it was from a residential property and routed the call away from the commercial team to the residential unit.

All these issues and many more came pouring out through the journey mapping session. And apparently, they'd all been raised with the management and leadership teams but the employees stated that "nothing's ever been done".

TIP
Ask your employees how proud they are about the experiences and memories your organisation creates and why that is.

So not only did customers have an experience that was diametrically opposed to the "warm welcome" in which the brand had invested so much money, their employees were completely disengaged. When I asked them about how they described their roles to friends and family, a number even said they'd make something up or they'd rather say they were unemployed.

As for the engagement survey, employees had indeed been giving nines and tens but only because they thought a high score would secure their annual bonus. The leadership team was shocked, but they now had a depth of insight they weren't expecting and committed to sorting things out immediately. All from a couple of customer journey mapping workshops.

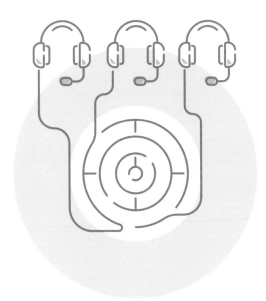

Is the Customer Experience the exact opposite of the mission statement?

One last benefit – journey mapping is fun. Seriously, have some fun. It's far from being a dry exercise and is a great way to foster employee engagement. They're on their feet adding value, not being talked at. They're being asked for their opinions, to role-play personas and to think creatively. They're asked to think about different scenarios and "What if …?" ideas.

Look at a journey mapping workshop as you would a Customer Experience though. You want participants to come away engaged and enthused, telling everyone else about it. So if they get distracted, go off on wild tangents and have a laugh they're more likely to share the stories.

The noise and laughter in some sessions I've been in has been a real tonic. It doesn't, as some sceptics would believe, reduce the quality of the output. Before you know it you'll have more and more people wanting to join your movement and grow your cohort of advocates for what you're doing.

WHY BOTHER?

Customer journey mapping is probably the easiest starting point for anyone looking to improve the right customer experiences. That said, I still encounter business leaders who see it as a waste of time. They don't see it as a means to a very commercial end; to them it's about employees pretending to be customers and having fun with coloured sticky notes.

We know how journey mapping leads to better experiences, which in turn improve sales, revenue and retention. That alone, however, sometimes isn't enough to shake cynics out of the complacency tree. They'll say the business is making money, they have satisfied customers and employees know what they're doing; why change, why spend time doing what we call "journey mapping"?

They will often simply ask, "Why bother?" It's not easy when those leaders want instant gratification for any activity. We've looked at the benefits but we can flip the argument to see what would happen if we don't bother. What if we don't do journey mapping – will we miss out on anything? What happens if we don't try and understand what it's really like today and should be like tomorrow to be a customer? Well, here are just a few things that will happen …

TIP

If you don't map journeys, how can you empathise? If you don't empathise, how can you become more customer-centric?

There's no meaningful purpose

The mission statement and vision, the guiding princi-ples, should be about customers – not the organisation. Absent a real understanding of customers' needs, hopes and expectations a business can only operate in a vacu-um. There's no consensus around what should be done and why, so everyone will carry on doing their own thing, preserving the corrosive effect of silos. The sole "purpose" is to make money. The irony being, they'd make a lot more money if only they had a meaningful customer-oriented purpose.

We waste money on the brand

Pre-Covid-19 advertising expenditure was measured in the billions. Yet whether it's ten cents or a billion euros, those investments are wasted if the promises made by the brand are not backed up by the reality of the experi-ence. After all, the brand is what people tell each other it is, based on what they remember – not what the clever strapline says. And we all know what impact the pres-ence of broken promises has on a relationship.

We measure the wrong thing

It's easy to measure the most obvious things but is that simply a process audit of what the business thinks should happen? Journey mapping will highlight the things customers value the most; we need to know how to do what's most important. It also avoids employees feeling pressured to chase a number rather than feeling empowered to give the right experience.

We waste effort

Money, time and resources are all finite but one of the great things about journey mapping is that it is very helpful at prioritising what to do next. With a deeply empathetic view of customers it becomes a lot easier to challenge personal agendas, inwardly-focused projects or new products that fit into the "technology for tech-nology's sake" basket.

COMPLACENCY –
THINKING THERE'S
NO NEED TO DO ANY-
THING DIFFERENTLY
– IS EXACTLY WHAT
YOUR COMPETITORS
WANT YOU TO BE
THINKING.

Complacency eats away

The gap between customer expectations and reality is one of the key drivers of a sustainable business. A company may feel secure because there's no obvious burning platform. As consumers, we have exposure to many companies across a variety of sectors and so our expectations of better experiences are rising as quickly as our tolerance of poor ones are falling. Journey mapping would highlight that gap very clearly.

We miss a big trick

An essential component of effective journey mapping is to see it from the employees' perspectives, otherwise we have no idea how easy or difficult it is for our people to deliver the right experiences. They know about fragile processes, about broken hand-offs, about a lack of risk-free empowerment and inflexible policies. Their ability to deliver the experience is a link in the chain that can't be kinked or broken.

We hand over an advantage to competitors

Chances are, your competitors are mapping their customer journeys too, meaning they will be in a better position to take customers away from you. They are de-risking the sustainability of their business by understanding what their – and your – customers will respond to positively.

Journey mapping is invaluable in shaping what we should do, giving reassurance and confidence that we're on the right track. Whether your leadership team choose to act on your insights is entirely up to them. However, the better you're prepared the more facts and evidence you will uncover and your arguments for change will be irresistible.

You're about to create a catalyst for your movement, you're going to grow a band of followers and gain credibility for being the customer's voice that holds the leadership team to account. Let's get going and plan our first journey mapping workshop.   «

NOTES

CHAP

PREPARING AND PLANNING THE WORKSHOP

Your thorough and practical preparation now will pay dividends after your journey mapping sessions. In this chapter we'll look at objectives, the scope, who to invite and setting up the room. You need your workshops to be a good experience for your colleagues; your reputation and the longevity of a successful CX programme depend on it.

PREPARE WELL. EXPECT THE UNEXPECTED. MAKE YOUR WORKSHOPS THE TALKING POINT OF YOUR ORGANISATION.

We've got the green light to "do some journey mapping". That's great. Or, you've just decided to get on and do it anyway and see who'll join in. Either way, we're at an exciting stage.

Okay, where do we start? There's no doubt that done properly, customer journey mapping provides rich insights into what it's really like to have a customer or client experience and what we should do to make it better. In the right hands, it's an effective tool that's being used more and more. Personally, I've lost count of the times I've been in a meeting and there's a cry from the back of "We'll need a customer journey for that!"

It's great that organisations are putting themselves in their customers' shoes more than ever before. What's not so great is that many of those "journeys" turn out to be existing linear process maps, operational flow charts or decision trees.

To be the one to drive your organisation's journey mapping programme is a fantastic opportunity. It can also be a little daunting, so this section of the *Playbook* is all about planning and setting up your first workshop.

You'll find you need to ask a lot of others. You'll be put in a position where you need to convince them they should take part. You'll need busy colleagues to find time out in their schedule to attend workshops. You'll need to make time with the leadership team, their gate-keepers and other colleagues you may not yet have met. You may need access to information the data and in-sight team guards jealously.

You therefore need a clear plan. We've already seen the benefits you can talk to stakeholders about. In this section of the book therefore, we'll start prepar-ing the groundwork for your workshops. Here are a few straightforward questions to pose before we can put sticky notes anywhere near the wall.

PLANNING FOR SUCCESS

1 — What are your objectives?

What do you not have today that the journey mapping will give you? How do you want things to be different? Why now? Of the benefits we covered earlier plus those specific to your own situation, what are the top three you're aiming for?

2 — Who will you invite?

If it's your first workshop you might opt to invite members of your own team. As your confidence in running the sessions grows, you will need to cast your net wider, spending time recruiting stakeholders from across different functions. Consider too those from commercial partners, outsourced operations; anyone who has a role or influence in any step of the journey you're about to map is a potential attendee.

When it comes to inviting the CEO or someone from the leadership team, only you will know if they might have a stifling effect on the levels of engagement. I would absolutely encourage you to have a senior colleague open your workshop, perhaps drop by during the day and then wrap things up. It's important that your group sees and hears from the top how this work links to future fortunes of the organisation. It's also your moment to shine, to be seen as the one for giving real traction to your Customer Experience movement.

As eager as they might be to join in though, if a leader's presence will mean others in the group feel intimidated, say only what they think the boss wants to hear or just withdraw completely, then limit their involvement on the day.

An obvious group to have in your session are customers themselves. My own experience is that more often than not it's better to leave them out of your workshops.

You'll need to go into your workshops with a good idea already of what the key pain-points are and, absolutely, customers need to validate what you have done. However, in your session you'll be having hugely important conversations where colleagues learn about their own business, its processes and each other's work. They'll be asking questions and there'll be a few surprises along the way. Some will know things, others won't, and myths will be created or exploded. It's all invaluable but they are not the sort of conversations you want to have in front of a customer.

As with having a senior colleague with you, some attendees might feel awkward about sharing real issues, how processes are held together by goodwill, string and sticky tape.

If your journey is highly specialist or technical then there is a case for having customers present. For example, cinemas, airports and shopping centres ask disability groups and charities to come in and help with their journeys.

TIP
It seems counter-intuitive but if this is your first journey mapping session don't feel under pressure to have customers present. Create your journey with colleagues first, validate later.

In most cases though, I would suggest leaving customers until you can show them something you're confident they will recognise.

3 — How many attendees?

The methodology works just as well with a handful or a mass gathering. Your numbers might also be limited by the location you'll use.

To start with though, you might run a test workshop with three of four friendly colleagues but for a typical session the sweet spot is around 12 to 16 participants.

That's a manageable number if you're hosting on your own. It also allows you to garner many different perspectives and split into two groups to map the journey of two personas. If you have over 20 show up, that's a great sign of the engagement you have but allow a little more time for introductions, settling down after breaks and questions.

Whoever you invite, be sure to explain how much you appreciate their input, what they can expect and what's in it for them. We've looked at some of the benefits already, but your ongoing stakeholder management will lead to your knowing what buttons to push for different people.

Why should staff bother? What good reason can they give their manager to take time out? Bosses like to think their people are indispensable and, for sure, operational challenges will be ever-present. It's why supplementing your own efforts by leaning on supportive senior leaders to endorse what you're doing is so important.

4 — Where?

The appropriate environment will make a big difference to your day. If you can, choose a location that has plenty of space, light and flat walls. I know from my own experience that having people tripping over themselves in a hot, windowless room isn't conducive to a relaxed, productive session. Likewise, when your groups are putting sticky notes up onto the paper on the wall, it's not helpful if it's wrapped around radiators, pillars and window frames.

If you are planning to include a walk-through of a premises, will anyone need a pass to enter areas for which they wouldn't normally have access? Be sure to let people know you're coming too – it sounds obvious (it is) but having a group of attendees armed with cameras and notebooks descend on an unsuspecting cleaner or security guard is not likely to end well.

TIP

Ideal numbers might be up to 12 or 15 onsite, up to 6 or 8 online. But, if you have more people who want to join you, stay flexible and find a way to let them in.

5 — Homework?

Before the workshop you can reassure everyone that they don't need to do any preparation work. That said, it will help if they can at least give some thought to relevant customers' and employees' issues they are seeing and would want to raise.

What do you know already about this persona and journey? What data and insights do you have that will add to everyone's knowledge about them?

6 — Presentation and workshop materials

We often learn the hard way, or is it just me? In preparing for your workshop you'll most likely have a presentation deck on your laptop to guide everyone through the day. As this is centre stage for your performance, ensure you have access to other copies of it.

It's still a refreshing surprise to simply turn on my laptop, connect it to the local network and within seconds see the slides on screen behind me. Too often though, and it happens to this day, we arrive in meeting rooms where, so it transpires, no external laptops are allowed

Be prepared; your supporting slide deck should not just be on your laptop but on a memory stick and in the Cloud too, just in case …

BATTLE BOX

⊘ Contact names and numbers

⊘ Travel documents and directions

⊘ Sticky notes of various colours

⊘ Roll of white paper

⊘ Scissors

⊘ Putty/tack

⊘ Sticky tape/duct tape

⊘ Phone charger and leads

⊘ Adapters for laptop and VGA/HDMI leads

⊘ Laptop power lead

⊘ Spare notepads and pencils

⊘ Stubby whiteboard pens

⊘ Knife and screwdriver

⊘ String

⊘ Sweets or fruit to give your energy levels a boost

to be connected to the network. The connection might be made but no combination of pressing HDMI-this and AV-that will break through the deadlock. So have your deck backed-up at least on a memory stick and in the Cloud should you need it.

Nearer the day itself you'll pack your "BATTLE BOX" of bits and pieces. Not everything always goes to plan so being self-sufficient and prepared will keep your sessions flowing nicely if you have to interrupt proceedings. Waiting while someone wanders off to find sticky notes that actually stick, a sharper pair of scissors or a battery for your presentation pointer saps any momentum you've worked so hard to establish. Opposite is a checklist. Some things you might never need ... but you never know.

WHICH JOURNEYS TO MAP?

This is another fundamental question, the answer to which needs absolute clarity before you get anywhere near your workshop. Not least, because it will have a bearing on who you invite. Believe me, if you try and get everyone in the room to agree on this one at the start of your workshop, you'll be there a long time.

There are two component parts to this: we need to clarify WHO (the persona) is doing WHAT (their journey). It is the combination of these two things that creates the experience.

Exactly who is the customer?

To improve an existing experience or design a new one we must have genuine empathy with those on the receiving end of what we do. Traditional segmentation approaches that give us Millennials, Gen-Y, "socially savvy", "wealthy with no kids" and so on are helpful but only to a degree. Data-hungry Marketing machines will, for example, assume that everyone who lives in the same postcode or was born around the same time will follow similar behaviours. It's simply not true.

TIP
Be crystal clear on the scope or your output will be diluted; define exactly who is doing what.

For an organisation wedded to metrics, processes and projects, commoditising customers in that way may feel more comfortable. Yet it fails to highlight that we're dealing with real people who interact with us because of or despite their own back-story. They have different motivations and are looking to us to improve their lives in some way, not just sell something.

We need personas to paint a more accurate picture of who our customers are. When we understand what they want and need from us, their hopes, fears and expectations, we have a clearer sense of how we fit into their lives. It's the flipside to a subconscious but flawed assumption that they are happy to comply with the processes that we've built and that suit us.

I've seen personas run to 20 pages of a PowerPoint presentation. They look more like a novel that just ambles through someone's life. My preference, and recommendation, is to create something much more succinct. You need your journey mapping audience to take on the characteristics and mindset of the persona, perhaps for only a couple of hours or a day. You're not asking them to be method actors preparing for a six-month run on Broadway.

Aim for a stable of around six personas to begin with. They will have plenty in common, especially the basics (everyone expects to be treated with respect) but there will be characteristics that clearly differentiate them. Your family of four will have different expectations from a student. The carer of someone with a disability will have different needs from a "high-flying executive".

In a workshop, focus on just one or two personas at a time. I usually provide a one-page summary in the workshop and then give attendees a few minutes to get to know the persona. They can discuss it, adding any relevant information they think will help to become immersed in their alter ego's world.

A couple of frameworks I use are shown in the boxes.

TIP

Personas, not Marketing segments, are invaluable in helping colleagues understand quickly and succinctly the role the company plays in customers' lives.

CUSTOMER PERSONA

What do our customers want, need, hope, fear and expect?

OUR PERSONA'S NAME IS	THE JOURNEY THEY ARE ON IS	THEY ARE (BRIEF DESCRIPTION OF RELEVANT FACTS)	THEIR IDEAL OUTCOME FROM THIS JOURNEY IS

THEIR MOTIVATION FOR THAT IS	WHAT THEY HOPE FOR IS	WHAT THEY'RE WORRIED ABOUT IS	WHAT WOULD REALLY FRUSTRATE THEM IS

CUSTOMER PERSONA

Example for a corporate in-house General Counsel

I DON'T SUFFER FOOLS GLADLY. DON'T START YOUR PITCH BY SAYING YOU'VE BEEN ESTABLISHED 100 YEARS. I KNOW THAT ALREADY. I KNOW YOU DO LAW. TELL ME WHAT MAKES YOU DIFFERENT.

NAME: LAUREN DORDER
JOURNEY: SHE'S CONSIDERING APPOINTING A NEW LAW FIRM

MOTIVATIONS

▷ I'm under pressure to link what I do to the bottom line; we can create efficiencies by refreshing the panel
▷ I want to bring new thinking to the business
▷ I'm new here and can use this process to prove myself

GOALS

▷ To have a law firm that acts as part of the team
▷ To have them contribute as a strategic partner at least cost
▷ Make me look good

PAIN POINTS

▷ I don't want any surprises in the billing
▷ You need to demonstrate what extra value you bring
▷ The stakes are high: keep your promises, every time

STRONGEST EMOTIONS

▷ Hope
▷ Anxiety
▷ Overwhelmed

By bringing customers to life as a person, not a segment, we can show the rest of the business what's most important to them and why in a meaningful and engaging way. Give the persona a name, draw a picture of them or a day in their life. Take time to discuss what they think, say and do.

We're talking here about customers but personas can – and should – be used equally for employees, stakeholders and partners when you come to map their journeys too.

In business-to-business sectors apply a little lateral thinking about who the "customer" is. I worked with a global credit card company that provided its customers with cards on which their employees paid travel expenses. When I asked the credit card company who their customers were they reeled off a list of well-known brands. After a bit of nudging they acknowledged the customer was actually a person, so most likely a CEO, the IT Director or Chief Financial Officer. In other words, whoever signed off the purchase and renewal orders.

More nudging later and it dawned on them that while the CEO was indeed a key customer persona, so too was the customer's employee checking out of a hotel on the other side of the world. If the system was down, they were in an awkward position. Likewise their IT manager, who set everything up and oversaw the programme on a day-to-day basis. And a few internal customers such as the Customer Success Managers who were the bridge between the two organisations.

Mapping those personas, each with different needs, fears and expectations forced the credit card company to look at itself from a previously unseen perspective.

What specific journeys are you going to map?

Just by taking the number of customer, employee and stakeholder personas, multiplied by the reasons they each might interact, multiplied by the ways they interact and multiplying that by the number of your different products or services they might purchase, the permutations can run into the hundreds if not thousands.

There are so many to choose from. Do you pick the ones you're most familiar with? The ones that generate the most complaints? Then we need to know what is the customer trying to achieve? What do they need? What difference to their life will it make?

TIP

It's quite likely you can map dozens of journeys. Be patient, prioritise strategically and be prepared to grow your library of maps one by one.

Taking time now to find clarity will pay huge dividends in the future. We can't afford to focus effort on something that isn't really a problem or an opportunity. If that happens, not surprisingly, people will drift back to their day job and next time we mention "Customer Experience", eyes will roll sceptically.

Get it right, though, and you can share compelling stories that reshape the corporate mindset and behaviours. You build a narrative around what it's like to be a customer and you'll prioritise your interventions with greater confidence, knowing where to take out unnecessary costs and where to innovate.

The journey scope could be at a holistic level, encompassing everything the customer does with you. This is often referred to as the ─○ "END-TO-END" JOURNEY. Personally, I would discourage the notion that our customers' relationships have a finite start and end point. The concept is that it's their journey and we will drop into and out of it at various points. They have events in their life that eventually lead them to us and they will hopefully remember us long after they've bought their last widget. Their "experience" is therefore still very much alive beyond their interaction with us.

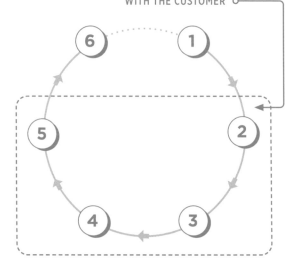

END-TO-END JOURNEY
(CAR HIRE)

1 — I'm planning my holiday

2 — I'm checking my car hire options

3 — I'm booking it

4 — I'm collecting the car

5 — I'm using the car

6 — I'm reflecting on and sharing what it was like with friends

COMPANY'S DIRECT INTERACTION WITH THE CUSTOMER

A true end-to-end journey

Alternatively, the journey scope might be something narrower such as making a complaint or changing profile details on their online account. If you're unsure and don't have specific issues to explore take a wider approach first. As you document the things your customers do, think, see and hear you'll be identifying smaller journeys that can be unpacked and mapped in their own right.

So the exact persona/journey combination you choose will depend on a raft of considerations. The first journeys you choose will depend on your own circumstances. It may already be clear but if not, here are a few things to consider to help focus on what works for you:

You know instinctively

The one(s) you've been thinking about as you read this; the proverbial burning platform. Where is the investment in your brand promise being undermined? What is the issue everyone talks about, or worse, the one everyone just dismisses as a barrier "because it's always been that way". If you could map only one journey, what would it be?

Which customers do you want more of?

Use the insights from your data to identify which customers or partners are most valuable to you. Where does your revenue come from? The most profitable? The most likely to be active advocates? Work backwards from there, understand what they value and what the nature of their journey with you is.

High profile or political issues

It may not be a customer's most significant journey but there's an internal imperative for getting this one right. While the platform might not be burning as such, you know beneath the surface it's smouldering and could ignite at any time. Showing your stakeholders the customer's perspective will help nudge them into action sooner rather than later, reducing the associated risk and snuffing out any complacency.

TIP

If you've no obvious burning platform to focus on, think about how your customers' expectations are changing, set by other brands they deal with. How might you need to adapt? If you still get complaints, why is that?

Be guided by your purpose, ambitions and CX strategy

Your values, strategic intent and corporate objectives will direct you to where your priorities lie. How does today's journey compare with what it should be, ideally? Where are the gaps between today and how good you want to be? For example, if you set out to be "Earth's most customer-friendly business", you might look for the journeys where customers have the greatest direct interaction with your people.

Complaints, customer feedback and operational metrics

An obvious consideration, but your data analytics and qualitative feedback will be a good signal of where to focus effort. However, we know most unhappy customers don't complain so don't ignore the journeys where there may be less obvious signs of frustration. You should also consider mapping the journey of when a customer complains or goes to the effort of giving you feedback, positive or negative.

Look beyond typical customers

Thankfully we're not all the same but processes tend to assume we are. For example, people with a disability and their families need to interact with the environment you create; I've often seen that if we get things right for people with a physical or cognitive disability we get it right for everyone else too. And how do you deal with customers who are apoplectic with rage? They might be spitting blood because of the downward spiral created by your processes rather than because they are simply nasty people who deserve to be ignored.

Not just customers

Employees, partners, third parties and stakeholders will all benefit from having their journey mapped. For example, it might be you can map a Customer Success Manager's experience of getting a new client up and running. Or map what it's like to go through your recruitment process to what Day 1 looks like. If your employer brand talks about being a "meritocracy" or simply a funky place to work, mapping out the journeys gives you plenty of evidence and stories to showcase your promise.

TIP
Journey mapping is very versatile; as well as for customers, it works for employees, internal and external stakeholders, in B2B environments and can even be adapted for objects such as a wheelchair through an airport.

IF YOU ARE TO EARN THE RIGHT TO HAVE CUSTOMERS COME BACK, BUY MORE AND TELL OTHERS TO DO THE SAME, THERE'S NO TOOL QUITE LIKE JOURNEY MAPPING TO PROVIDE A RICH CUSTOMER UNDERSTANDING.

Still not sure?

Get your team together and jot down the typical interactions a customer has with you over the life of your relationship with them. Organise them by themes and in chronological order. Some may last months or years; others may take minutes or seconds. Make a list, choose the first one to pick off and see where it takes you – it has to be better than doing nothing.

With a lot of thought and plenty of preparation you've decided which journeys to map, whose experiences they will be and who will join your workshops. You've done the schmoozing to get everyone there, you've managed stakeholders well and your cohort of attendees are looking forward to joining you.

You're now ready for the journey mapping workshop. «

PART 2

RUNNING THE WORKSHOP

CHAP

THE WORKSHOP

The excitement is building and we're ready to showcase what we do! Your colleagues have arrived, the room is set and you're in charge of how the next few hours go. Facilitation can be straightforward, but this chapter will show how to stay on your toes and how to keep everyone moving in the same direction to ensure you get the most value out of your time together.

JOURNEY MAPPING WORKSHOPS ARE HIGHLY INTERACTIVE; SHARING STORIES, LEARNING ABOUT THE COMPLETE JOURNEY, DOCUMENTING THE IDEAS AND OBSERVATIONS.

This is the point at which you walk into the room you'll be using for your session and you begin your pre-performance routine. It's a critical but often undervalued period but, as any good chef or surgeon will tell you, how you prepare now will have a significant bearing on what happens next. It will be obvious to everyone if you've just arrived two minutes before they did. We're all about Customer Experience and so here is the opportunity to put the final touches to your "attendee experience".

The set-up on the day

There's a lot riding on how this session goes. Not just for the credibility and impact of your CX programme but for you personally as the individual driving that agenda forward. A journey mapping workshop is one of the most visible and tangible parts of Customer Experience and directly engages people right across the organisation with your message. For the reasons we've already discussed, a workshop can therefore have a huge influence on the future levels of buy-in from your colleagues and leadership team to the whole concept of Customer Experience.

FIGURE 2

Three stage journey: In this section we look at the hour or so before the start of your journey mapping workshop.

BEFORE	DURING	AFTER
PLANNING	FACILITATING	ACTING
Preparing journey mapping sessions to ensure they're strategic and effective	Running workshops on the day, keeping them on track	Analysing what it all tells you and using it influentially to drive change

The colleagues who'll be with you today need to feel everything is professional, structured and relaxed. Your preparation is how you demonstrate your empathy and respect for the fact that they've taken time out of their diary to join you. Some will have jumped at the chance and are excited. Others are cringing because they've got so much work to do and they hadn't planned for this workshop. A few will have been told to attend and are wondering why on earth they are there.

The point being, the stakes are high.

Journey mapping workshops are a very high-profile statement of intent. You want people to be energised and on board when they leave and join your growing band of CX champions around the business. You want them to go back to their boss and say, "It was brilliant, very interesting to get the customer's real perspective on what we do. We should stay close to the CX team and support them so they can support us. Can't wait to do it again!."

Remember this is your very own Customer Experience, where your colleagues and, to a degree, the success of your CX programme, are your "customer". Give those who come along a session to remember for all the right reasons. It needs to work efficiently, to demonstrate how it can support their own work and to be a catalyst for your organisation's commitment to CX. Time spent in these workshops is invaluable in creating excitement about what you're doing and why. Inject your personality, accommodate theirs, be professional – but make sure to have some fun along the way too!

Many of the suggestions for the immediate time period before your session are obvious. That said, nervous energy can do strange things to our rational mind. The better the setup, the better the day and its ongoing impact. I know from my own early experiences that the opposite is true; turning up in a flap and rushing to get everything set up hardy fills everyone with confidence. You want participants to want to be part of your team and help get others engaged with what you're doing. Thinking and planning ahead is so important.

So, your alarm goes off and the day of reckoning is here. Be excited and look forward to it. You've planned well, engaged everyone you need to and you have everything covered. Let's do this!

KNOW YOURSELF, KNOW HOW
BEST YOU CAN RELAX BEFORE
THE WORKSHOP BEGINS.

On your way there

You've already done your "reccy" so you know where you're going and how you're going to get there. I often use breakfast or travel time on the way there to have a final run-through of my opening comments. How will I introduce what we're going to be doing? How do I make sure it's relevant to the audience?

Once you're up and running you'll be fine but be clear in your head about what you'll say first. By now you will be able to visualise and articulate exactly how your day will unfold, why it's important, everyone's role in it and what happens next.

Be really clear in your mind what three key messages you'll give right at the very start. Don't leave it until the last minute to plan unless you're genuinely superb at winging it. Of course, you may need to make some final adjustments based on extra information someone gives you or there's a topical event in the morning's news you can reference. However, err on the side of caution and assume you won't have any thinking time as you set up. Get those opening messages sorted well before you arrive at your workshop.

Arriving

If it's your first time, arriving at the location for your workshop there will understandably be a few eager butterflies. If you've done it before and you've done your preparation, that's just the excitement kicking in and showing how much you care about this!

As you open the door into the room and turn on the light, the stage for your performance is revealed. The sense of anticipation grows, so while you have the room to yourself now is the time to get set up.

Get to the location early. Not only does it make the journey there less stressful, especially if it's a new location for you, it gives you longer to get to know your surroundings for the day. I'd recommend you allow an hour to dress the room, get yourself into the right headspace and have time to chat with your colleagues as they arrive. Thirty minutes should be ample to get everything ready, then you have the same time again as a contingency, to get some air before you start and to meet people as they come in.

While you potter sorting everything out, ideally you'll have the space to yourself with no distractions. However, be mentally and physically ready for that to not be the case. You'll find that some people will arrive early, sometimes even before you if they've travelled a long way. So be comfortable wrestling excitable rolls of paper onto the walls and thinking ahead to what else you need to do while others are watching you, talking to you and generally coming and going.

Your role is to make people feel welcome and excited about what's ahead. So even though the day isn't yet formally under way, your relationship-building with those you'll spend the day with is. It's also a great chance to source some candid views on the journey you'll be mapping. Listening to conversations through the day is key, and it can start even before you've begun.

Once you've done it a few times you'll be in a slick routine, your prep leading up to this point will pay off and participants will be impressed with how you get on with things.

TIP

People might arrive early and watch you set up. Don't get flustered, engage enough so they feel part of the day already but keep ploughing on with your set-up.

Dress the room

This is where you turn a generic meeting room into a real journey mapping workshop. I usually think about this point of the day in three sections; the walls, my laptop and the "accessorising". It doesn't matter in which order you attend to them but I usually focus on the walls first; as people arrive, it's easier to welcome them and engage if you're plugging in a laptop rather than reaching up high to stick things on the wall.

I pre-cut my large strips of paper the day or so before the workshop into 2.5m lengths. They are generally 70cm wide so I have two strips which will go one above the other to give enough space for the myriad of sticky notes you'll have.

You'll need one set of materials per persona. If you've seen the room before, you know exactly where your sheets of paper will go and where people can group together in comfort. You might be able to put sticky notes straight onto a plain surface or glass, but I'm assuming here we'll use the paper we cut out in the preparation stage.

TIP
Have as much pre-prepared as you can. It'll look professional and save you time just when you might need it.

BE PREPARED FOR THE UNEXPECTED

If the location is new to you, be ready to think on your feet. I've arrived onsite where the room I'd been allocated had been handed over to someone far more important. Rather than a light, airy space with plenty of flat wall surface, I was in a small, dark Tudor library. Lovely oak beams and a vast collection of books but no windows and not a flat surface in sight. So, despite having my paper pre-cut to length I now had to find time to quickly cut it again to fit the panelling and doubled up the thickness to provide a small degree of a flat surface. I worried that people would find the uneven surfaces frustrating but the reality was that they just got on with it. So, faced with the unpredictable, "Keep Calm" as they say and do the best with what you have.

I've also seen room set-ups that appear rushed at best, impractical at worst. Some things look obvious in hindsight but can be valuable lessons for first-timers, for example: ─○ THINK IT THROUGH ○──────

It's important to make this look professional. Quick and agile? Yes. Informal? Sure. But not scruffy. Little things count. If you do put crisp white rolls of paper up on the wall for the sticky notes, make sure they're nice and flat. Like pulling a bedsheet taut or trimming a racing yacht's sail. One of the fundamentals of CX is about how we make people feel so if it looks like we couldn't be bothered to prepare thoroughly and present everything in a respectful way, what does that say about you and the whole credibility of Customer Experience?

If you have handwriting like mine then you'll pre-print the journey map headings onto the appropriately coloured sticky notes. Simply create the headings on your laptop, put sticky notes on a sheet of A4 paper into your printer, align it all and you're ready to go. When they're put on the white paper you immediately create a professional visual impact for everyone when they walk in the room. There's also now a massive clue for them right there about what they're going to be doing!

THINK IT THROUGH

Don't put the paper on the wall next to a doorway that's being be used. Obvious, as I say, but not only can it be dangerous, it's also a real distraction for those in the room when they are pouring their energy into thinking about the customer journey. Groups tend to spill out into a wider circle as the day goes on, so give them as much room as you can.

Remember not everyone else might be as tall as you. If attendees need to stand on a chair to put their sticky notes on the wall, you're creating an environment that's not only unfair to them but you've increased the chances that they'll disengage from the process altogether.

TIP
Attention to detail and keeping things neat adds to how professional people think your session is.

Have all your props out and ready. If you're using any handouts such as your persona profiles, have them where you can get to them quickly once you get into the day's proceedings. There's nothing worse than seeing someone forget an important bit of the day then watching them spend five minutes floundering around trying to find where they put the "really important stuff". Create your basecamp for the day in a nearby corner of the room and know where everything is.

One certainty is that during the day the team will come up with some great ideas and questions. Even if they are off-topic we must hold on to them. To do that, allocate a couple of flipcharts as an "ideas catcher". Or, allow space across the bottom layer of your journey map with the heading "What if …?" Tell the group that if they have an idea or burning question to jot it down on a sticky note. No detail needed, no "Yeah, but we can't do that because …". That idea can be explored in time; the important thing is to catch it while it's fresh.

If your journey mapping involves a walk-through of a location, such as a visitor attraction or an airport, then it is imperative that you check out the route before your groups descend on it. Does everyone there know you're coming today and do they know why? Do they know it's not a witch hunt and that you're not looking to point fingers of blame at staff when things don't go well? If you need special access passes, are they all sorted? Will you need to do that before your workshop starts on the day?

All the while you're setting up the room, be prepared for any last-minute changes. Someone might say the start is delayed – or brought forward – half an hour. The room you're in might need to change because there's been a double-booking of the space. Such things happen but if you've already given some thought to it, you'll react with all the professionalism and calm people expect.

Starting bang on ─○ TIME is often a challenge. There's ○─ always someone who can't get there for the start, sometimes for perfectly legitimate reasons, sometimes for dubious ones. There will be others who simply drift in just after you're supposed to start. It's down to you to start when and how you think it appropriate but if you're at risk of starting late, keep an eye on signals from those who did arrive at the appointed hour. If you're in any doubt, it's more respectful to them to start than wait for someone who's "just sending a couple of quick emails".

TIMING

Timing can be an issue in keeping things on track but generally we can control and flex it as we go through the session. It's not like we are with the ultra-disciplined RAF's flight display team, the Red Arrows. At their briefings, everyone is there in good time, without fail. As the start time approaches, the mood shifts from general chit chat to the Squadron Leader counting down on a synchronised wrist-watch, "5-4-3-2-1-9am-Morning everyone. Today we're ...". There's no waiting for someone who's decided to grab a coffee. There's no delay because the laptop won't plug into the TV screen. We're not the Red Arrows so, as much as we'd like to, starting bang on time rarely happens. It's easy to lose 15 or 30 minutes from the schedule before you know it.

Don't panic about getting under way late. Have a Plan B ready if you need to claw back lost time as you go through the day. Shave a few minutes off the exercises here and there, limit the conversations that go off at a tangent or shorten break times a little and you'll get things back on track.

All the preparation is done and we're about to start. Enjoy the moment of your Customer Experience. Give those who come along a session to remember for all the right reasons. They want it to work efficiently, they want to enjoy it and see how your thinking and methodologies can support their own work. Be proud of what you're doing too, it's taken a lot to get to this point. You're going to pour high-octane fuel on your organisation's commitment to Customer Experience and raise levels of interest, engagement and excitement about what you're doing.

The room is dressed, you've a full cohort of people ready to share their thoughts. It's time for the curtain to rise, to get everyone's attention and for your moment to shine. Let the workshop begin.

TIP

Be really proud of what you've done to get this far. The next few hours will fly by but keep focused on why you're doing this.

CHECKLIST
THINGS IN YOUR ONE-HOUR PREP

✓ Fix the sheets of paper to the wall and
   put the journey mapping headers in position

✓ Get any props, handouts and the sticky "voting" dots
   ready and make them easily accessible

✓ Provide pens and sticky notes at each
   journey map area in the room

✓ Check you know where the toilets and refreshments
   are as well as emergency exits – any fire alarms
   expected today?

✓ Check any videos in your deck work with sound

✓ Have your opening remarks absolutely clear
   in your mind

✓ Be proud of and excited about what
   you're about to do

We're now at the point of the most tangible element of journey mapping, the workshop. You might be running it onsite in a training room or using an online video-conferencing platform because of the Coronavirus pandemic. To avoid confusing the issue, this section assumes you can hold a "traditional" workshop and meet in person, even if that means adhering to new post-Covid-19 rules. I look at how things might be different online later but by and large many of the principles apply however you run the session.

Facilitating a customer journey mapping session for the first time can be daunting. However, assuming you've invited the right people from across the business, and those who said they'd come do turn up, you should have an audience eager to get involved.

Keeping it flowing and on track is no small challenge. As they used to say in the *Dukes of Hazzard,* expect the unexpected. For some of your attendees there may be urgent operational issues they need to go and sort out. The big boss might need to have an unscheduled call with them. Some people will feel they must be seen to be important so won't stop tapping away at their keyboard. There will always be at least one person who is

BEFORE	DURING	AFTER
PLANNING	FACILITATING	ACTING

Three stage journey: Keeping your sessions on track

there because they've been told to attend but have no idea why or what to expect.

It's easy to get distracted but if you stick to your plan, give participants absolute clarity about what they are supposed to be doing and make it an enjoyable experience, you'll be heading in the right direction.

Here, then, are a few suggestions for making sure your time with others is going to generate the compelling insights you need and that you become famous as the go-to person for anything to do with Customer Experience.

THE DAY'S AGENDA

You have a lot to get through so your session needs to be structured and managed.

In your preparation time you will have set out a timed agenda. Here's a suggested agenda with approximate timings if you are running a session over a full day. You will need to add in your breaks, with no more than 90 minutes or two hours at the most between them.

TIP
Create a structured, timed plan but be prepared to flex it.

TIMED AGENDA

🕐	15 min	Welcome and introduction
🕐	20 min	Strategic context
🕐	20 min	What do we mean by Customer Experience?
🕐	15 min	Share your own stories
🕐	20 min	Meet the personas
🕐	20 min	Journey mapping – Stages
🕐	40 min	Journey mapping – Doing
🕐	40 min	Journey mapping – Thinking
🕐	30 min	Journey mapping – Feeling
🕐	40 min	Journey mapping – Our views
🕐	25 min	Journey mapping – Metrics
🕐	20 min	Play back the stories
🕐	10 min	Vote
🕐	20 min	Conclusions, questions and next steps

While you should manage your group's expectations about how the day will run, I'd suggest you keep the specific timings for each element to yourself. You'll need to advise them of the finish time and when you plan to break for lunch but, as we've discussed, it's highly likely the steps in between will need to flex and change. There may be parts of the day the groups fly through, there may be bits they need more time on or you may have an interruption.

As you go through the day keep an eye on your timings as, however you divide up the schedule, you still need to finish on time. Reinforce that message, especially when you have your breaks, as it's very easy at that point for your attendees to wander off.

This is only a suggested outline for a one-day session. You know your people and organisation best so adapt it as you need to. However, sticking to the agenda opposite as an outline, let's go through the workshop from the beginning.

Welcome and introduction

Remember, not everyone in the room may be as passionate about CX as you are. Your preparation work will have identified the varying degrees of enthusiasm for your session. Some people may be there only because they've been told to go by their boss and haven't a clue what they day is about. Some may just want you to get on with it. And others may think they've seen it all before and have a "What's the point?" attitude.

They can be a tough crowd and while I don't doubt your ability to win them over, here's where you can borrow authority from as senior a leadership person as you can persuade to come along to open proceedings.

As the "host" you can welcome them on stage but even just a couple of minutes from the boss sends very clear signals that it's important stuff and everyone should get involved. It also says to the team that they have permission from on high to take time out of their busy schedule to attend this workshop. The attendees will also be conscious that the senior representative has – or at least should have – noted their participation and their willingness to contribute.

TIP
Your natural charm and passion for the subject will get the group on your side but if you can, have a leader attend to open the session – the more senior and supportive the better.

Should the senior leader stay or go?

It will depend on your culture and the personalities involved. More often than not though, my advice would be that having got everyone engaged and relaxed, senior management should retreat and let you get on with it.

I've seen first-hand how their presence takes the momentum out of the energy you've created. However well-intended, even in small, family-run businesses as well as large multinational corporates, having them hang around stifles the very conversations you need to be flushing out.

Some people have the confidence to look into a CEO's eyes and tell it exactly as it is. However, although others may have the same views, they would rather feed them in via a third party – you.

By all means invite bosses to pop in to check on how things are going or stop by for lunch. At the very least, having them come back at the end of the day to hear the highlights and biggest issues is preferable. Bear that in mind as you go through the day – if the CEO puts in an appearance just as you're wrapping up, what are your immediate top three messages? That will also begin your thinking about what it all means and what you do next.

TIP

Remember that the CEO may well put in a surprise appearance and ask, "How's it been?" Think about what you are going to say. What are your immediate top three messages? What surprised the team? How were their levels of engagement? What did they learn? What's the elephant in the room you've all been talking about?

HOW'S IT GOING?

Stay alert and keep a Plan B ready in case of losing time through interruptions or distractions

HAVING THE CEO OR ONE OF THE LEADERSHIP WELCOME EVERYONE IS A REVEALING WINDOW INTO JUST HOW CUSTOMER-CENTRIC THEY WANT THE CULTURE TO BE.

Even though you've briefed senior management, the likelihood is that a well-placed reminder the day before your session won't go amiss. Remind them that it's not just about putting sticky notes on the wall. It's a great opportunity to reinforce the vision and then hear views from all corners of the business about what things are really like and to collaborate on how things might be different.

Interestingly, their performance in opening your show will give you a good insight into whether their commitment and passion for the role customers play in the business matches the aspiration and vision. It doesn't happen often, but I've had more than one senior management team member – including CEOs – turn up, trot out their rehearsed lines with no emotion and, with absolutely no conviction, declare that "We-put-customers-at-the-heart-of-err-everything-we-do".

Your journey mapping therefore offers a view of the real culture. Simply putting up posters around the office that speak to being a "great place to work" is not a solution or way to drive engagement. The impact of what your leaders do and say cannot be underestimated.

TIP

It's a great opportunity for the boss to step up and show everyone how committed and excited they are about being more customer-centric. Make sure they get their time in the spotlight.

If you do have a lacklustre experience, politely but quickly usher the boss out of the room. Hand out your box of chocolates and fruit, get your crowd talking again, bring their energy levels back up. You have to step up to be the true Customer Experience leader and while your attendees may not have noticed, you now need to get things under way.

Introductions and the dreaded "icebreakers"

Unless you have a cast of thousands, go round the room and let everyone have their moment in the spotlight. Not only is it the right and polite thing to do, we also shouldn't assume that everybody in the room knows each other. They rarely do, so here's a big opportunity to tick a big box and sow the seeds of new relationships.

However, this bit has a habit of being either too brief or too drawn out. If your attendees spot an opportunity to get away with saying as little as possible, they will. All you'll get is a name, a job title and a shrug of the shoulders as if to say, "That's it, that's me. Move on."

At the other extreme, asking everyone to tell a story eats into your time. In one of my first sessions I thought I'd try and relax everyone into the day by asking for

TIP

Introductions are important – it may be the first time people have met others not just from the same organisation but who also have involvement in the same customer's journey.

USE YOUR JUDGEMENT FOR HOW LONG YOU SPEND ON INTRODUCTIONS.

their name, role and then two facts; one true and one a lie. The others had to guess which was which. Yes, it was fun and we certainly learned a lot about how everyone's mind worked – but it was too much time off-topic.

In the next workshop I replaced the truth or lie element with asking everyone to share a brilliant or shocking customer experience they'd had in their own personal lives. It led to some thought-provoking conversations, but again took too much time.

Attention started to drift and it was difficult to pick up the pace and focus again. So I then did the "Tell us about your own experiences" section as part of the context setting a little later, which we'll come to shortly.

The temptation is to get through the icebreaker as quickly as possible. A good middle ground is simply to pause and engage briefly with each person. Make one quick observation or ask a question about their role and how they might have a direct or indirect link with the Customer Experience. If they struggle to make the connection, then ask about their internal customers.

It's a bit of an investment in time at the start of your session but what this approach gives you is material and anecdotes to refer back to throughout the day.

It keeps everyone involved and provides real life examples to provide the context of why you're doing this work.

Strategic context

The point of this part of the workshop is to answer the question, "Why are we doing this?" Without an overarching narrative your journey mapping will be fine but risks solving the wrong problems because it has nothing to guide it in the right direction.

It doesn't need to take long but anchors the work firmly in the path of your overall vision. If, for example, the ambition or brand values include "to give the world's warmest welcome" and "make customers feel they're part of our family" then that gives a solid benchmark against which to highlight where things are falling short or where there are already great examples that need protecting.

Use statements and soundbites from what your organisation has already produced. It may be comments by the Board in the annual report about how important customers are. It may be a brand value about what customers can expect.

Actions speak much louder than words though. Calling out these statements of intent from the annual report, masterplans or strategic investors' updates not only gives you context for your journey mapping, to see how close or not you are to them, but it is also a great way to then hold the leadership team to account. If you uncover experiences that force customers through hoops just because it's better for your contact centre's processes, you can say to the CEO: "If you're genuine about making our customers feel welcome then we need to change the processes." Or, "Let's take down that poster that says 'We put customers at the heart of everything we do', because we don't."

By inference, it also vividly highlights the absence of a simple statement about the role you want to play in customers' lives that everyone can get behind. If you don't have a Customer Experience vision, now's the time to create one. Or at least use your work to inform management of what it should be.

Assuming you have a CX vision though, having set the scene about where the business wants to go, now is the time to show how important Customer Experience is in getting there.

TIP
Journey mapping shines a bright light on the stated corporate ambition – is it genuinely customer-centric or a convenient soundbite?

"If you're genuine about making our customers feel welcome then we need to change the processes."

CEO

Explaining Customer Experience

At the start of this *Playbook* we looked at what we mean by Customer Experience and how it differs from Customer Service.

It's important to run through this at the start of your session as you need to help your group out of their day-job mindset. They need to spend most of the day thinking like one of your customers – but that's easier said than done. Taking a few minutes early on to explain just what Customer Experience is and how it works at your organisation is time well spent.

Including the wider ins and outs of Customer Experience at this stage would turn this book into volumes. There is no shortage of writing on the subject so for now, we'll stay focused on journey mapping. After all, your attendees only need to hear things at a high level.

If you're in a CX role you will draw on your knowledge about the principles of Customer Experience to create a couple of relevant slides to talk your audience through. If you need inspiration, one model you can refer to is that any Customer Experience is made up of three core elements – FUNCTION, EASE and EMOTION. It's a great set-up for your next section, where you ask participants to recount their own stories and experiences.

TIP

Holding a CEO to account can be uncomfortable but if they are authentic about improving things they'll be glad you did.

"Let's take down that poster that says 'We put customers at the heart of everything we do', because we don't."

Their stories

Ask the group to think about any good or bad experience they've had recently and discuss it with the person next to them. Ask them to explore those three perspectives, function, ease and emotion – did the "experience" work, was it as expected and is it consistent? Was it easy or did they have to jump through hoops? And how did it make them feel? Exploring what happened, why that might be and the consequences often creates real "Aha" moments. As participants realise they are going to look at their own business in the same way, the penny drops.

Your available time will dictate how long you spend on this. You might ask just one or two people to share particularly memorable experiences and have a quick discussion about them but I would steer clear of asking everyone in the room to tell their ─○ STORY. You simply won't have time but you can recommend that they do that exercise with their colleagues in future team meetings.

TIP
Get the group into the right frame of mind by asking them to share their own stories first.

STORY-TELLING

At the end of the workshop, and as you go about your daily role being a CX professional, you'll earn a reputation for telling stories and encouraging others to do the same. In one business where I worked, I was known as "Jackanory Jerry". (*Jackanory* was a popular BBC children's television series running from the 1960s to the 1990s, where stories were read before bedtime.) I've been called a lot worse.

Meet the personas

In the preparation stage we decided which personas we would focus on, creating new ones if they were needed.

It is now worth taking a few minutes for the group to get to know them. It's also the point at which you can split the workshop into smaller groups, each taking on a different persona.

Share your one-page summary of the persona's backstory, needs, hopes and expectations. Ask the teams to discuss what the persona needs most from you, what would be the icing on the cake and what they would find frustrating or perplexing. What else should the profile include?

We're not "role-playing" exactly but we are trying to immerse ourselves in the customer's world. Familiarising the group with the personas sets everyone up for the rest of the workshop and in my view is a non-negotiable element of the day. You know you've got it right later on when you hear colleagues correcting themselves, repeating your mantra that "it's not about our processes, it's about their experience".

THE JOURNEY MAPPING FRAMEWORK

Journey mapping is all about organising the thinking so the framework shown in ›Figure 3 overleaf is the one I use. It's straightforward and simple, yet effective at getting to the heart of the real issues.

This version of the journey map is for the "current state" – that is, what does today's experience look like? In Chapter IV we'll use an adaptation of the map for future experiences.

Having spent time getting to know a persona, we're now in a much better position to think like they think when they're doing business with us. The first two "layers" record the journey stages and what the persona does in each stage (Their Journey). Then we dig deeper into the experience of that journey by describing what they think and feel (Their Experience).

The last two layers allow the teams to revert to their day jobs and be themselves again. We ask what their views are and what they know, think or wish is measured (Our Experience).

TIP
At its heart, the journey mapping framework helps organise the thinking into manageable chunks.

FIGURE 3
The journey map will be built layer by layer

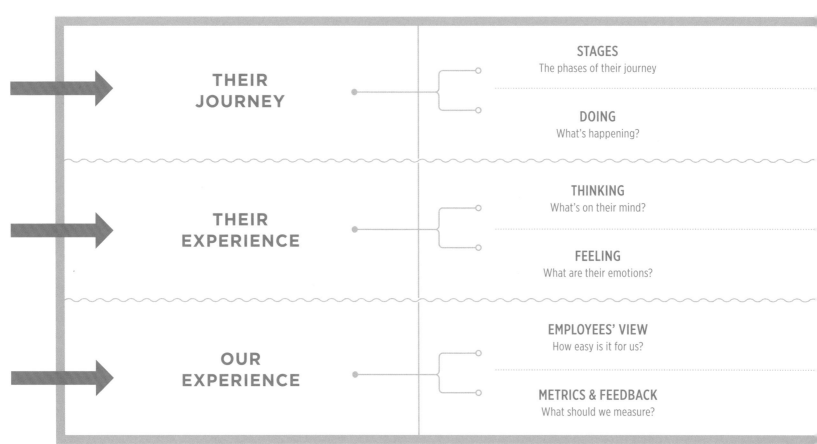

THEIR JOURNEY

STAGES
The phases of their journey

DOING
What's happening?

THEIR EXPERIENCE

THINKING
What's on their mind?

FEELING
What are their emotions?

OUR EXPERIENCE

EMPLOYEES' VIEW
How easy is it for us?

METRICS & FEEDBACK
What should we measure?

①	②	③	④	⑤

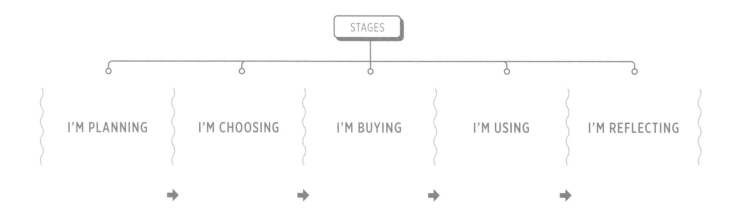

Stages

This is all about dividing the journey into manageable chunks, the "stages". We're looking for between four and six stages; too few and we won't see the wood for the trees. Too many and the chances are that the stage is something more tactical and should become a "Doing".

I encourage my teams to think about it as breaking the journey down into the *Before, During* and *After*. You could use the analogy of chapters in a book or scenes in a film.

Once you give them the order to start thinking and writing, you'll be jumping around from group to group checking they understand what they are doing. The worst thing you can do right now is slink back to check your own emails and leave them feeling stranded. I've been on the receiving end of that approach and it gnaws away at all the good you've done so far. If participants have any element of doubt about the process, you must nip it in the bud.

Depending on how well you think your groups will handle this step, you might need to give them a helping hand. As part of the preparation work in defining the journey to focus on, you most likely started to create the stages in your mind anyway. Alternatively, nudge things along by showing them what, at a generic level, the stages could look like, for example: ─○ GIVE THEM A HEAD-START IF THEY NEED ONE.

USING THE CUSTOMERS' LANGUAGE

Always encourage the use of "I" statements. It forces the team to think about what their customer would think and say, using their own language and not the organisation's language.

A rail operator was reviewing its customer journey for business passengers. However, it hadn't quite shaken off the habit of taking only an internal perspective. The stages they identified initially were straightforward and logical but very much inwardly-focused. They felt the stages of the customer journey were:

▷ Book and pay
▷ Using station estate
▷ Onboard and Sales (Embark – Alight)
▷ Customer Services

GIVE THEM A HEAD-START IF THEY NEED ONE

I ran a workshop programme where colleagues found it tricky to find the starting point. In their enthusiasm or apathy, they would either go straight into the detail of the journey or struggle with one over-bearing personality whose opinion side-tracked them from the job in hand. To give them a rolling start I took the most likely stages from the previous groups' work and had them written up and put on sticky notes before they'd even begun. They were given the opportunity to challenge and change the starting point but it avoided them stumbling at the first hurdle.

The language, often antiquated, was clearly not the same as their customers would use. It was based on their operations and organisational structure and, as a consequence, focused on just fixing broken and existing processes.

It was better than nothing, but a subsequent assessment of the journey flipped the perspective. By looking at things from the business passenger's standpoint the stages of the journey were updated and took on a whole new meaning (›see Figure 4).

> ▷ I'm making arrangements
> ▷ I'm travelling
> ▷ I'm at the meeting
> ▷ I'm going back
> ▷ I need help

TIP
Always remember, it's about their journey not your processes.

Forcing the business to use its customers' language in this way made it understand how it fitted into their world. They realised they weren't always directly involved in this customer's journey. The business persona had a meeting request for which they had to make plans to travel, which may have been arranged by someone else. The data might record two separate trips but in that customer's head it was just one journey to Manchester and back. When they were in their meeting, they were not on a train but they were thinking about what would happen if the meeting overran.

It was this sort of approach, thinking like their customers, that led to an Eastern European rail operator to establish a tie-up with Uber. With one ticket (digital, unlike the multiple pieces of identical paper we have to sift through on some UK rail networks), a ride would pick you up from the office and take you to the station. The train would whisk you to your destination where another ride would drop you at the office. And then the same in reverse. Functional, easy and relaxing?

Absolutely.

FIGURE 4

One customer journey, two perspectives

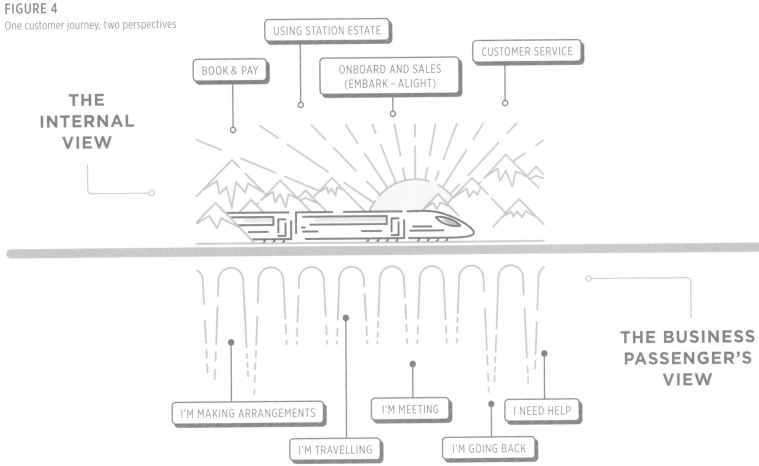

THE INTERNAL VIEW

BOOK & PAY

USING STATION ESTATE

ONBOARD AND SALES (EMBARK – ALIGHT)

CUSTOMER SERVICE

THE BUSINESS PASSENGER'S VIEW

I'M MAKING ARRANGEMENTS

I'M TRAVELLING

I'M MEETING

I'M GOING BACK

I NEED HELP

CUSTOMER

DON'T FORGET TO INCLUDE THE THINGS YOUR CUSTOMER DOES IN THIS JOURNEY THAT MAY NOT INVOLVE YOU DIRECTLY.

As your teams make a note of the stages it may also be helpful to add a timescale to each one. Some may only record a matter of minutes or hours whereas some, if the subject of your exercise is taking out a mortgage for example, will be measured in weeks and months. Either way, it will give more context for your colleagues and stakeholders who may not be customer-facing and who may not have quite the same understanding of what it's like to be a customer.

Doing

With your stages set out across the walls, you can now move on to the next layer.

We're going to ask the teams to think about what their persona physically does in each stage. This may be via your touchpoints or in their own lives. Just because the personas do something where there's no contact with you doesn't mean it's not part of their journey.

While looking at what the persona is doing, explore their motivations too. What are they trying to achieve, what is their "job to be done"? What's their ideal outcome?

Bear in mind that some of the activities noted in the "Doing" section might be journeys in their own right, worthy of investigation. For example, in the "I'm using" stage our persona may discover there's a fault. If it's flagged up as being important, reporting it can be mapped as its own journey in future.

Thinking

In this section we really need to get inside our persona's head. Ask the team to write down what they believe the customer is thinking at each stage of their journey. Your prompting questions for them might include:

▷ What does the persona think about what they see and hear?
▷ What unanswered questions do they have?
▷ What would they be saying to each other?
▷ What's bothering them?
▷ What are the pain-points, niggles and frustrations?

Based on their backstory, what they are doing and their motivations, they might be saying to themselves:

▷ I wonder if …?
▷ I hope/expect that …
▷ I need them to …
▷ I worry that …
▷ I wish …

Feeling

The combination of what the persona does and thinks is what drives their emotional response. There's no shortage of evidence about the hugely important role that emotions have in driving behaviours. The favourite question for any sports commentator or TV presenter is "How are you feeling?" It's a totally open question but the response and the reasons for it give you a direct and invaluable window into that person's life.

Ask the team to make a note of what emotions the customer is going through in each stage. They can just write the words or have a bit of fun drawing a cartoon or an emoji. Chances are there will be a real mix of emotions depending on how things go. We get excited if we're in a position to upgrade our mobile phone handset but then we get a sinking feeling about the processes we have to go through to get there. Capture all of the emotions to show the range.

TIP
"How does it feel?" – it's the go-to question for sports commentators and TV journalists to really understand the person they're focused on. It's the same for us too.

Our views

The teams stay in their groups but it's now time for them to revert to being themselves rather than inhabiting their persona's world. We're trying to discover their views on what makes the experience for customers better or worse. The questions you pose for discussion might be along the lines of:

TIP
Asking employees what they think about the leadership, culture and processes can dig deep into the psyche of the organisation. It may raise some awkward issues but that's why we're here.

▷ What helps employees and what gets in the way?
▷ Do they think the Board and senior management are serious about this whole Customer Experience thing?
▷ What processes are only held together with string and sticky tape?
▷ What happens only because of the goodwill of the teams rather than behaviours of the leadership team?
▷ What processes should change and what tools, information or resources do they need?
▷ Do the bosses listen when told what should be improved?
▷ Is everyone clear about where we're going as a business and why?

And so on. This section can open those cans of wriggly worms, so be prepared. If there are passionate or conflicting views be ready to moderate, keeping the lid on things while getting to the heart of the issues. It might be uncomfortable but that's partly the reason for this exercise. If it does become tense, be pleased, because without your workshop and intervention those problems may simply continue to fester.

Metrics

Any successful Customer Experience programme is reliant on the right qualitative and quantitative insight being captured in the right way at the right time. It must be analysed thoroughly and the evidence used to drive change, otherwise there's no point.

You and your colleagues will have an instinct for where things are going well and what needs improving. Making the case for some changes is straightforward and requires little more than a dose of common sense and a proactive "Come on then, let's do it" mindset.

However, what you discover through your journey mapping may mean that if the organisation is to be true to its vision and brand promise, it has some big

decisions to make. Not all – but some – may need financial investment, diverting capital spend away from other activities. You might be asking for a divisional head to release two people to help you or for them to push your priorities above theirs.

We look at influencing styles in Chapter IV but there's nothing like reliable and timely data to give you the facts and evidence you need. Sadly, while many businesses are awash with data there may be only so much that's helpful. Therefore this last layer in our journey mapping session asks the teams to make a note of:

▷ What they have already in terms of customer measurement at each stage of the journey, and
▷ What they think they need to fully understand the experience.

It's often the case that most customer measurement (the scores and reasons for the scores) is done at the end of the journey. Before then, much data will be an audit of operations, though we should include them if they are giving us an indication of performance.

Replay the story

We're closing in on the end of the session and you'll find energy levels starting to wane. Keep your engagement high in whatever way works best for you as you need to keep the participants' momentum going to the end.

At this point ask one or two attendees to tell the story they've just created. They should summarise the key points, the standout moments and the surprises. The purpose is to highlight what they as a group feel is most important to the other team. In the next section, you'll ask everyone to vote for their favourite idea or observation.

Take it from me that you need to manage their time closely. Be clear that you just want the key messages. You don't want them reading out every sticky note or you'll be there forever. At the end of a mentally draining day it's the last thing anyone needs. Take a cook's timer with you and set it for five minutes.

Voting

Your session will have created a wall that's plastered in comments, ideas and issues. They may number into the hundreds, more if you're doing a series of workshops over several sessions. You need some way, however basic, to capture the mood of the room and let attendees tell you what they think is most important.

Giving everyone a set of sticky dots seems a bit playful but there is a serious side to it. You leave the session with a clear proxy for what colleagues feel should be tackled next. When you're asked afterwards what you're going to do next, you've been given a clear mandate.

There are no hard and fast rules for this exercise. I use sheets of sticky dots and cut them into strips so everyone has at least six or seven dots with each one representing a "vote".

Ask everyone to get out of their seat one last time and cast their votes, putting the dots on the sticky notes that represent the ideas or issues they feel are priorities. They can put them all on one if they feel strongly about a particular issue and they should save a few to put on the other team's journey map.

Give people no more than ten minutes for this activity but as they do it, look out for where there are clusters growing. Summarise what they have voted for and then use the last few minutes of the day to wrap things up.

A simple idea to help find the priorities is to give each person sticky dots. Ask them to place their 'votes' on the things they think should be addressed first

Closing

Before everyone rushes for the door thank them for their time and contribution.

Call out a few highlights from the day and take any questions. Be ready for the one that is always asked – "Will anything really happen as a result of this?" I can't answer that for you. You can, though, reassure your group that you have the ear of the leadership team and that they've asked to see what you've done. The very fact that your session took place and there are more conversations being had about Customer Experience has to be a good thing.

Explain what happens next and what you are committing to in terms of action. There's no harm either in asking participants what they'll commit to in support of your work and the organisation's overall approach to customers. If nothing else, get them to spread the good word about how enjoyable and informative the day has been. They are now officially enrolled as your ambassadors and CX champions!

TIP
When you draw the session to a close be ready to explain what happens next. If you don't tell people, someone will ask you.

IT MIGHT BE THE END OF THIS WORKSHOP BUT IF IT'S TO BE TRULY EFFECTIVE AT DRIVING CHANGE, THE JOURNEY OF JOURNEY MAPPING HAS ONLY JUST BEGUN.

FINAL THOUGHTS OF THE DAY

It will be a long day, for you especially, so good preparation will make your life a whole lot easier and everyone will have a better time. Remember, you want them to go and tell their boss how good it was on so many levels.

You're leading the session but immerse yourself in the conversations and process too. There is so much to learn from listening to discussions about the issues, which may or may not be documented on the day. You need to be alert to those little nuggets of gold throughout the workshop.

WRAPPING UP THE SESSION

When you've finished your summary, secured everyone's commitment to being part of your gang and thanked them for their time, there is often a rush for the door. People have other commitments to get to, so don't take it personally.

Don't, however, rush the dismantling of the room either. What you have on the walls and in the scribbles around you are the foundations for your next step – writing it all up and influencing stakeholders to take action.

TIP
Immerse yourself in the day and your colleagues' thoughts. Listen to their conversations and understand their opinions. Have three stand-out messages ready for when you meet your boss and CEO next.

Take photographs of the journey maps before touching them. Unless you have a huge desk back at the office or walls where you can stick the journeys back up, it will be easier to write them up from photographs.

Make sure, though, that the notes don't overlap each other and hide what's written on them. While you'll still have the original to refer back to, it's much easier to sort it now and save time later.

In the enthusiasm to put ideas up on the wall, the sticky notes may not sit in perfect alignment with the stage headers. Another way to make life easier when it comes to writing up the notes is to draw vertical lines on the paper to delineate the different stages around the notes. Again, it might seem obvious right now but in a couple of days when you're writing it all up you don't need to be wasting time wondering if a specific idea belonged in the "I'm browsing" or "I'm buying" stage.

Another reason for photographing them *in situ* now is that the process of taking them down can set free some of the notes. In the same way we went for colour-coding the sticky notes, having photographic evidence will help trace the origins of a note if it becomes separated.

As we mentioned earlier, it's also helpful to have a visual record of what you did. Pictures of the team huddled around a colourful wall full of ideas and sticky notes immediately conveys the sense of the collaboration and engagement to those who weren't in the room on the day. It gives you collateral, too, for marketing your next workshop, to help manage expectations and get people excited about being part of your movement.

Last chance to clarify things

Before taking the journey maps down, have a quick scan and see if there are any notes that carry acronyms, something you're not familiar with or if something is illegible. If there's anyone else left in the room, ask them to clarify it while it's all still fresh.

TIP
Take the chance to clarify things immediately or at least in the day or so afterwards. It's important to keep the momentum going.

REMOTE WORKSHOPS

During the latter stages of the writing of this *Playbook*, the world came to an abrupt but temporary halt due to Covid-19. Offices emptied and for those still in a position of employment, working from home was the norm rather than the exception.

A central pillar of this book has clearly been about getting teams together in a meeting room or training suite for the journey mapping workshops. They were at their best when the banter bouncing round a room full of engaged people was turned right up and when everyone jostled to get their ideas posted on the wall. Many new relationships were forged over competition to see who'd grab the sweets first.

Happy days. But for good reasons, social distancing, an intense focus on hygiene and new, yet-to-be-fully-understood work practices mean it may be some time before journey mapping workshops are back to how we've come to know them.

Ironically, journey mapping will be as important as ever in understanding what the new world looks and feels like for customers and employees. Bringing colleagues together from across various functions, their

COVID-19 CHANGED OUR WORLD. OUR THOUGHTS REMAIN WITH CX PROFESSIONALS AND OTHERS WHO HAVE LOST SO MUCH.

interaction and conversations are still absolutely necessary if a company is to become and remain customer-centric.

One thing the Covid-19 lockdown gave us was confidence in running meetings virtually. If we weren't already, we quickly became familiar with platforms such as Teams, Zoom and GoToMeeting, to name but three.

Thankfully, journey mapping via video conferencing is very much a credible alternative to being together physically. In reality, it always has been, but few will have taken that option in favour of meeting in person for such an interactive session. In the short term it may be the only choice we have but as we learn and become more comfortable with how to run workshops remotely it may well be the norm. One day we may look back and ask ourselves, "Remember when we all had to travel to the same place at the same time? How old-fashioned!"

The core journey mapping structure will stay the same but not surprisingly some of the logistics will change. Remote workshops still allow the gathering of colleagues to share their views and to collaborate easily. Indeed, employees who are geographically distanced and for whom logistics prevented them from attending previous sessions, can join in without the cost and hassle of travel.

TIP
Ironically, one thing the pandemic gave us was the confidence to run journey mapping workshops remotely. It's different but it can be done.

How it might be different

If you're hosting your own journey mapping session there may always have been a few nerves. An anxiety about who to invite, whether they will be given time out to attend and how they'll contribute on the day.

Those things will most likely be no different but we now have the added dimension – and possibly more anxiety – of hosting the session in a virtual environment. Fear not – with a little preparation again things will be just fine.

Here are some points on running workshops in a virtual environment. ─○ THREE KEY POINTS first. «

THREE KEY POINTS FOR JOURNEY MAPPING IN A VIRTUAL WORLD

1 The usual rules about **keeping to time,** having an agenda, involving everyone still apply.

2 Keep the **numbers manageable.** Whereas you might be tempted to fill the "room" with as many people as want to join you, we need to keep things under control. You need to make sure everyone is with you during the day and they all know what they're doing.

I'd put an upper limit of around ten, which is enough to generate content and engagement but also allows you to have breakout rooms. Many more than that and keeping control, keeping everyone engaged becomes unwieldy.

In a busy training room, it's easy for those who want to, to slip to the back and let everyone else do the heavy lifting. Even more so in a virtual environment.

3 Break the workshop into **shorter time frames**. A virtual workshop lasting a day is asking a lot of anyone. Sound out your team, but a series of 90 minute or two-hour sessions may be just as productive and more tolerable (you want them to want to come back and do it again, of course).

Running workshops in a virtual environment.

MORE POINTERS FOR REMOTE WORKSHOPS

HOMEWORK

In times gone by, with the luxury of a day spreading out before you, some of the agenda would have been explaining tasks and helping attendees understand what questions they're answering. In a virtual world a little homework goes a long way. Send a note to your group in the lead up to the session; manage their expectations about exactly how the agenda will flow and get them to start thinking about the specific issues you want their views on. What you don't want in the workshop is people who've been distracted by their cat or a doorstep delivery then looking at each other through their laptop screen and muttering, "Eh? What are we doing?"

2

FAMILIARITY

If it's your first online workshop find a way for everyone due to attend to try out the technology beforehand. Before the workshop you'll be keeping them updated anyway, so use one of these messages to include a link to a test meeting. It ensures they can access the platform, their cameras are in the right place and they are at least familiar with the mute and video on/off buttons. The more faffing around you can avoid on the day the better, as the risk is that you'll be ten minutes behind before you even start.

1

ONE PERSON, ONE SCREEN

Everyone should be remote, to create a sense of balance among the group and avoid creating cliques. If some of the team are able to be onsite in the same building then get them to join individually from their desk space, a small meeting room or work from home.

3

GALLERY VIEW

Although it's your voice they'll hear most, whenever you're not showing a slide or working on a virtual whiteboard, use the Gallery mode to show all attendees rather than have your face dominate. Again, it helps create a sense of being together in one "room".

5

VISIBLE FACES

Make it a hard rule that everyone must be on video. Seeing faces and body language is crucial at the best of times when you're facilitating a workshop.

4

BREAKOUT ROOMS

Just like the real world, tools like Zoom allow attendees to go off to a separate space, work on their own group tasks, come back and share what they've done. It takes a little setting up, confidence in managing their expectations of how long they have left and the discipline to stick to the plan. To help, you can ask one person in each group to be the leader for their breakout session and they marshal their team from within.

6

Don't be afraid of hosting the session in
a virtual environment

VIRTUAL WHITEBOARDS

When participants break into smaller persona-based groups or groups to look at a specific part of the journey or idea, you need a practical way to capture their thoughts.

You'll need your judgement on this one about what will work best, depending on the platform you use. As a default position you can create a blank version of the journey mapping template in PowerPoint/Pages or Excel/Numbers. The purpose-built collaboration tools like Mural and Smaply are great and allow the work to be exported afterwards for write-up. Alternatively, use one of the proprietary tools that come with platforms like Zoom, Teams and GoToMeeting. Some allow smaller teams to each work on a specific space on one master version. If that's the case, make sure everyone has enough "elbow room" and they're not distracted by seeing others' comments popping up. You will need to orchestrate the return from the breakout "rooms" and then ask each team to shares its findings, but you can reassure them that you'll save the information generated and write it all up into one, shareable document afterwards.

7

PRESENTATION

Your audience is used to looking at your workshop slides on a floor-to-ceiling projected surface or a large flatscreen TV. They've now swapped those for a pop-up window on their laptop or phone. Use fewer words, appropriate typefaces (the usual suspects, Garamond, Franklin Gothic and Helvetica), bigger fonts (at least 24 points, larger when you can), more visuals and so on.

8

NOTES

PART 3

WHAT NEXT AFTER THE WORKSHOP?

CHAP

ACTING

The end of a workshop is just the beginning of the most important phase of journey mapping – acting on it. We need to understand what the priorities are, how we validate them and how we convince the powers that be to make customer-led changes. In this last chapter we'll help to define what happens next to keep your programme of journey mapping alive and adding value.

WE NOW NEED TO CREATE VALUE FROM THE JOURNEY MAPPING; WHAT NEEDS CELEBRATING AND WHAT NEEDS CHANGING?

The sessions went well, everyone was engaged and the team is bursting with ideas and enthusiasm. You added extra value by creating an environment where people from across all functions shared their behind-the-scenes stories. In doing so they learned a lot more about their own business, which wouldn't have happened without you. All in all, it's a good result.

And there's more. We've added to our cohort of CX champions, we've created high expectations and we're armed with new and deep insights about what it's like to be a customer. We are poised with the evidence about what will make a genuine difference.

However, here we face the biggest risk to our customer journey mapping; nothing more happens. Don't let that be because of you. Being a CX professional is often about having perseverance and resilience, no more so than right now.

There are many reasons why journey mapping is threatened by being derailed or curtailed. A shift in focus might come in the form of an overwhelming day job full of other priorities, an apathetic leadership team or internal politics.

BEFORE	DURING	AFTER
PLANNING	FACILITATING	ACTING

Three stage journey: As you unplug your laptop, switch off the light and
leave the workshop, your attention turns to what happens next

To the uninitiated in your leadership team or among
colleagues, it may simply be in the name – a perception
that "journey mapping" is like a team-building, hap-
py-clappy away-day with no real purpose. Trust me, not
everyone gets it.

I've even had one "Head of" stick his head around
the door of a workshop he was passing and say, "When
you're done plastering my wall with colourful scribbles
can we get back to the real job of running the business?"
He wasn't joking. It shows how important it is to secure
early and broad stakeholder engagement.

The whole point is that journey mapping is about what
you do with what you've found and how you use it to
secure buy-in from those whose support and influence

**TO MAKE MEANINGFUL
AND LASTING CHANGE
YOU MUST GIVE YOUR
STAKEHOLDERS
CLEAR EVIDENCE,
REASSURANCE AND
CONFIDENCE.**

you need. We must provide unequivocal evidence about why we're losing customers and why complaints just cost us more money. We must give management confidence that if they commit any thinking time or change behaviours, let alone make resources, tools and information available, their business overall will be the stronger for it.

Your journey mapping workshop might be over but this journey you're on has only just started. To make meaningful and lasting change you must give your stakeholders clear evidence, reassurance and confidence.

The stories you can now tell about looking at your business from your customers' perspectives, about what it's like for employees, are invaluable in influencing change.

INFLUENCING CHANGE

If you are making the case for your customer-centric movement, then journey mapping is your Exhibit A.

We talked earlier about how journey mapping must be STRATEGIC, EFFECTIVE and INFLUENTIAL. Strategic, in the way it fits and contributes to the overall business. Effective, in the approach it takes to flush out the most actionable insights.

And journey mapping must be influential in helping others to "get it", to see the compelling need for change and for stakeholders to see what's in it for them. You are the catalyst for a movement behind which you need colleagues to be gathering, eager to play their part. That's what journey mapping is all about at its heart – influencing.

You can "borrow" authority from the CEO or a senior colleague. There are, however, only so many times you will win people over by saying, "We must make this change because XYZ says it's a good idea". It might have some traction for a while but it will wear thin, believe me.

Your position within the organisation's hierarchy can also be the reason people will join your gang. However, saying, "The company is paying me to be our Head

TIP
Your credibility is key to being influential. The journey mapping helps build a rich understanding of customer behaviour and its impact on the business like nothing else.

THAT'S WHAT JOURNEY MAPPING IS ALL ABOUT AT ITS HEART – INFLUENCING.

of Customer Experience so we should do this" has an equally short shelf-life.

Your biggest opportunity to influence lies in your "earned" authority. The more you immerse yourself in customers' lives through exercises like journey mapping, the more you have the credibility and evidence to secure the buy-in you need, the decisions and support you are looking for.

We've got people interested and we've flushed out some great initiatives. However, the reality is that whatever gold we uncover and however energised we feel, we have to make it a meaningful part of our stakeholders' work. We don't want it lost in the noise of their inboxes and meetings.

The end of the journey mapping workshops is just the beginning. There's a long, exciting journey ahead. It won't be easy but it will be incredibly rewarding. It's why we love being part of the CX profession.

So, what next? What can we do to make sure the path down which we've just started doesn't wind on aimlessly? When your workshops are done it's time for them to earn their keep. Here's my take on what your TO DO LIST is now likely to include:

THE END OF THE JOURNEY MAPPING WORKSHOPS IS JUST THE BEGINNING.

TO DO LIST

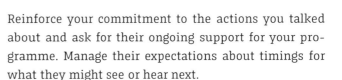

- ☑ Communicate straight away
- ☑ Document the journeys
- ☑ Validate the journeys
- ☑ Report with recommendations
- ☑ Customer measurement
- ☑ Share it with colleagues
- ☑ Future-state and Design
- ☑ Other journeys to map
- ☑ Map employees' experience
- ☑ Create the necessary governance

Let's take one step at a time.

1 — COMMUNICATE STRAIGHT AWAY

As they say, little gestures go a long way. First things first: the day after your workshop send a message to everyone who attended or supported your session with a note of thanks for their contributions. Highlight one or two standout messages from the day or amusing events to which everyone can relate.

Reinforce your commitment to the actions you talked about and ask for their ongoing support for your programme. Manage their expectations about timings for what they might see or hear next.

Overall, though, the purpose of immediate communication is to keep the momentum going and stay front-of-mind when participants are drifting back to their day jobs.

Another valuable message at this point is to your key stakeholders. To the line managers who released people from their teams to attend your workshop, a big "Thank

TIP

It's hard to overstate how important it now is to keep the momentum you have created going.

you". To the senior colleagues who you will be contacting in the coming days and weeks with your findings and recommendations, a quick update on how the sessions went, paving the way for your requests of support to come.

2 — DOCUMENT THE JOURNEYS

You will leave your workshops with rolls of paper and notes everywhere. They need collating and organising in a logical way to give you a robust foundation for the next stages of your programme.

My recommendation here is to take the journeys of sticky notes and recreate them in a shareable document. Whether you use PowerPoint/Keynote or Excel/Numbers is up to you. There are software models you can use but for the moment, keep things simple and simply write up the notes verbatim in a matrix format; list the stages across the top with the notes about what customers are doing, thinking and feeling, and your colleagues' views and measurement issues, in the appropriate place.

It's simple, it's visual and it's all in one place. Just as importantly, if you write it up yourself, you're immersed in the journey. You get to read every comment. You'll start to link issues, to define your themes and to get a sense of the priorities.

Having created the storyboard of the journey you now have a base proposition to work from.

Your document will be detailed and text-heavy, so consider creating a "lite" version for sharing. This may only have the top three comments for each stage/consideration section (for example, I'm choosing/doing or I'm using/feeling). You know the detail lying behind it but this will make it much easier to create an illustrated version of your journey map and take it to the next stage, validation.

3 — VALIDATE THE JOURNEYS

So far, your journey map is an informed view of your customers' experiences. Nonetheless it remains a perspective put forward by a relatively small group of employees. To ensure your findings and recommendations carry more credibility, we need further authentication from other employees and customers.

TIP

When writing up the journey you're not creating a work of art. It must look professional but don't focus on style over something that tells the important stories in the clearest, most compelling way.

This adds a depth of insight to test or reinforce what you have done. It will give you confidence that you're planning to make the right changes. Crucially, while much of what you can report already will resonate, it will mean you are no longer exposed to a stakeholder's challenge that your conclusions haven't been properly validated by a broader cross-section of employees and real customers.

TIP
Validation with customers themselves and other colleagues strengthens your reasoning for change and avoids sceptical stakeholders thinking you've taken only an internal view of the world.

Reaching a wider audience of colleagues will hopefully be relatively straightforward. Make good use of your internal communication and collaboration platforms by posting a note of the work you're doing. Share the high-level customer journey and ask for comments. Do colleagues recognise the key issues? What else is impacting the customer experience that should be highlighted? Even if you do not unearth any new issues, the act of engaging and involving them will be appreciated and you can demonstrate to stakeholders how you now also have company-wide input.

We discussed earlier in this *Playbook* how we would generally not ask customers to attend the initial journey mapping workshops. Their presence stifles the discussion and the unknown but gritty issues you need to bring to the surface are likely to remain unknown.

Creating a shareable version of your journey map is vital in telling the stories and building on what you have done

That said, it is now time to proactively seek customers' views. Arrange individual conversations with a number of customers onsite or via video conferencing. These will be individuals who match the persona profiles used in the journey mapping.

Invite them via email or your website to view the summary version of your journey map and ask them to comment. Strengthen the characteristics of your personas by talking to customers about their motivations, needs, hopes, wants, fears and expectations.

Make the most of your customer panel, if you have one – a group of customers who've said they're happy to help you develop new ideas and give honest feedback. If you don't have such a panel, now is a good time to establish one and make it part of your governance.

Alternatively, use focus groups if you can bring a number of customers together. Talk to them in overall terms about their experience, talk them through the map you've created and ask what they recognise, what's missing and what's not emphasised enough.

Even from just half a dozen or so interviews you will glean more useful insights and hear things in their language. All this puts you in a better position to make the argument for change.

TIP

Engage with your customers in a way that you can repeat in future. Explore how their voice can be part of your organisation's decision-making process.

PHONE CALLS, FOCUS GROUPS AND CUSTOMER PANELS — EFFECTIVE WAYS TO REINFORCE YOUR JOURNEY MAPPING NOW AND, IN THE FUTURE, YOUR OVERALL CUSTOMER EXPERIENCE PROGRAMME.

4 — REPORT WITH RECOMMENDATIONS

You're now in a position to prepare your report. This is the document that will be your supporting evidence as you inform stakeholders what the current situation is really like and what needs to be done differently.

Writing it up can take many forms depending on how you want to use the information. You might simply want to document the sessions for your own reference and create a shopping list of actions to work your way through. Or, you might need to produce a compelling report for your governance forum and the Board to review.

There's no single right way to do it so the exact structure of that report and whether you use PowerPoint/Keynote or Word/Pages will be whatever works for you. You might have one full version from which you create shorter adaptations depending on the audience and what you want them to do.

If your audience is time poor or is someone who says they "don't do details", then your approach might be to go straight in with "These are the three key conclusions and here is what we need to do differently". Your evidence and reasoning then follows – if they need it.

Alternatively, you may set out the process and findings more chronologically to ensure you are leading the reader down the path you want them to take.

Whichever approach you take, if stakeholders are to agree to providing you with support in whatever form that may be, the document needs to be influential and credible. It must be watertight and pre-empt their questions and motivations so it's not open to challenge from sceptical individuals. The report has to demonstrate how and why it's relevant to them.

Remember though, to make it your own, add your personality to it and include or ignore what's most appropriate for you. So here's a list of elements you might include:

▷ Introduction
▷ Definitions
▷ Context
▷ Methodology
▷ Findings
▷ Recommendations and actions needed

TIP

Your report documents what you've found and what the organisation needs to do about it. It will be at its most effective if it's done in tandem with your passionate stakeholder management, your perseverance and your squirrelling around the business to drive actions and change.

Introduction

A short reminder about what this work is all about and what you expect your reader to do or think as a result.

Depending on how you want your audience to receive the information, at this point you can include a succinct one- or two-page summary. It gets straight to the key messages and if your stakeholder doesn't have time to read anything else, they'll know what you want of them and why. Likewise, if they have any questions they'll let you know.

Definitions

TIP
Keep the report focused on the facts and the "So what?"

Your audience may have had limited exposure to the type of work you do or they might still need convincing about its value. If so, you can explain briefly what "Customer Experience" is, how it works and examples of companies that have benefited from being customer-centric.

A brief description of the principles behind customer journey mapping may also be worthwhile to set the scene for the rest of the report.

Context

Why is this work important? Why now? What is the corporate vision, strategic plan and commercial objectives in which it sits? How might the organisation be stronger because of the customer-centric actions you are recommending?

One powerful way journey mapping helps is in the way it can hold the leadership team to account for its existing mission statements and visions. If, for example, the vision is to be "The easiest company in the world to deal with", you can manage expectations here that the journey mapping will show how well – or not – that is being achieved at the moment, with real-world stories from the front line.

Methodology

Paint a picture of what you did and who was involved. Highlight the fact that you had X number of employees from across different functions attend Y number of workshops.

KNOW YOUR AUDIENCE AND ADAPT IT APPROPRIATELY. IT'S PART OF YOUR OWN INTERNAL CUS- TOMERS' EXPERIENCE OF YOU, AFTER ALL.

Explain the outline of your mapping sessions and how, beyond generating rich insights, they were designed to also bring teams together to create new relationships and to learn about their own business.

If you experienced your own built environment, include that too – you need to give the reader reassurance about the extent to which you immersed yourself in your customers' lives. If you have taken photos of the groups in full action mode – taking pictures as they walked through your stores or looking animated as they put sticky notes full of ideas on the wall – add those in too. It's a very clear and visual statement of the lengths you went to.

Findings

The point of this section is to highlight the reality of today's experiences for customers and employees – for better or worse.

Pick out your key observations and conclusions. If you have several, group them by themes to help your readers digest the information.

TIP

Share photos or a video of what you did to add reassurance about how thorough you have been. It also creates interest and helps recruit more people for next time.

Themes could be where there are implications for change, for example:

▷ Overall (issues affecting all personas and all journeys)
▷ By persona (irrespective of the journey they are on)
▷ By journey (irrespective of persona)
▷ For a specific persona and journey combination
▷ By channel, product or operational function
▷ Communications and information
▷ Employee experiences and training

As before though, you are best placed to decide which themes will be most relevant to your audience.

Be prepared to address sceptical stakeholders with uncomfortable truths or political sensitivities. Don't be put off. In fact, be encouraged because your mapping holds the evidence you need.

It needs to be provocative but constructive too. By its nature, journey mapping is looking to find ways of improving things. It therefore spends most of its energy and focus on experiences that are flawed, wrong, frustrating, inconvenient and unnecessary. To a sceptical reader there is a risk that the overall tone becomes negative. It's a core human trait to be defensive, so you want stakeholders to appreciate that you have flagged the issues in a constructive manner, not think you're just digging for problems or point scoring.

Two things help immensely here. First, a fact-based argument and secondly, the inclusion of a celebration of the good things too.

Your cast-iron arguments will come from what you and the teams observe on a day-to-day basis and what they discussed in your session about what they identified as an issue. Moreover, what they collectively voted on as being the highest priorities. To strengthen the case for change, add relevant data from the analysis of your insight and complaint root causes, and from unstructured feedback sources too.

Include photographs from your onsite tours, showing unequivocal evidence to make your point. A picture tells a thousand words and at a stroke will remove any denial that, for example, bins had not been emptied or café tables had not been cleared.

In one instance the company's leadership team looked at each other in surprise when they saw their own advertising was five years out of date (the sign read "New for 2016"; it was already 2020). Use screenshots

TIP
If you are to hold the leadership team to account, to ask the awkward questions and drive customer-led change, your arguments need to be absolutely watertight.

YOU AND YOUR
REPORT BUILD TO
A SET OF CONCRETE
ACTIONS THAT WILL
UNDERPIN THE
DELIVERY OF THE
CORPORATE AND
CX VISION.

or a user-experience video of your website showing how ambiguous it is or how many hoops customers are made to jump through.

Add into the mix your validation step, where you took the initial findings to customers and asked for their views. It now has its moment in the spotlight. Use the insights this stage gave you to add more weight to your arguments, to put it across in your customers' language and to highlight how the issue makes them feel and the impact it has on what they do next time.

So, you've given stakeholders an objective state-of-the-nation review. Now comes the part to which this has all been leading – your recommendations and actions needed.

Recommendations and actions needed

Be really clear about what you are proposing. A long shopping list of actions may be what is in your head but you'll need to be brief to engage your stakeholders and get them to buy-in to your list of recommended next actions.

You might present them in the same themes as your findings. There might be a "top ten" followed by the remaining wishlist. You will be challenged on how you've prioritised the chart toppers, so have your reasoning documented as part of the report. We look at the prioritisation process in the next section.

Another way to present actions is to consider the tactical (short term), strategic (medium term) and cultural (longer term) recommendations. Then, overlay that with who the action is targeted at – customers or employees.

Creating a visual representation of your recommendations in this way will help your stakeholders understand what you are asking for. For example, assume you have three signature actions in each (›see Table 2).

TIP
Too many recommended actions can be overwhelming. Keep to a few signature actions – small things with a big impact – to start with.

TABLE 2
Visual representation of actions

	TACTICAL SHORT TERM	STRATEGIC MEDIUM TERM	CULTURAL LONG TERM
FOR OUR **CUSTOMERS** →	Action #1 Action #2 Action #3	Action #4 Action #5 Action #6	Action #7 Action #8 Action #9
FOR OUR **EMPLOYEES** →	Action #10 Action #11 Action #12	Action #13 Action #14 Action #15	Action #16 Action #17 Action #18

To dig a bit deeper, add the rationale for the first level of detail for each action. I've used a recommendation to change the way customer feedback is measured as an example (› Table 3).

TABLE 3
Change to customer feedback metric

^^^^^^^^^^^^^^^^^^^^^^^^^^^^^^^^^^^

ACTION #1
CUSTOMER MEASUREMENT

THE RECOMMENDATION IS	to change our key customer metric from an advocacy score to one that tracks customer effort
THE REASON IT'S IMPORTANT IS BECAUSE	a customer effort score and the qualitative drivers behind that metric will give us a more accurate reflection of what it's like to be a customer doing business with us
IT WILL BENEFIT US BY	▷ gaining a better understanding of where and why our customers are having issues ▷ better indicating how well our brand promise to be easy-to-deal-with is performing ▷ increasing profitable business as a result
IT WILL BENEFIT THE CUSTOMER BECAUSE	the things we improve and introduce are then more focused on making things easier for them rather than just adding our new processes
TO MAKE IT HAPPEN WE WILL NEED TO	add the customer effort score into our insight programme, analysis and reporting we will also need to be comfortable in moving to a new headline metric, communicating it clearly and, for three months at least, running the old and new metrics in parallel to wean people off the advocacy score
LIKELY EFFORT ON OUR PART	minimal – mostly a quick change to how we ask for feedback and report the findings
LIKELY BENEFITS	significant for the reasons outlined above

5 — CUSTOMER MEASUREMENT

The many issues raised by your journey mapping will bring you to an exciting point in your own Customer Experience journey where you get to be a key influencer for customer-led change. Unfortunately, misinformed opinions, urban myths and politics can all stand firmly in your way.

We've already sought further qualitative validation for your report but one thing that's effective at breaking through cross-functional barriers is the right metric. Customer-based metrics provide hard, quantitative evidence of how the organisation is performing and how much stronger it will be as a result of a given change.

Metrics, measurement and return on investment are extensive topics and the subject of many books and academic studies. By and large these are outside the scope of this *Playbook* but your journey mapping does highlight two things we should take notice of; what we are measuring and when we should measure it.

Many organisations, if they capture a metric at all, will seek just one. It is taken at a point that's convenient to the business and its processes, not what's most appropriate for the customer. I've often discovered companies asking, "How likely are you to recommend us to your friends and family?" and obsessing over the score, not realising that it's not so appropriate for the B2B business they are in and that it's more of a brand score than product or transaction score. (› Table 4)

So it's key to get the measurement right to quantify just how good the journey is – or isn't. The "metric" stage of your journey mapping workshop asked colleagues what they knew about the customer's experience. That's why we continually reinforce the need to think from a customer perspective, not our own processes.

TIP
Measure what's important to customers throughout their journey, not just at the end of an experience that went well.

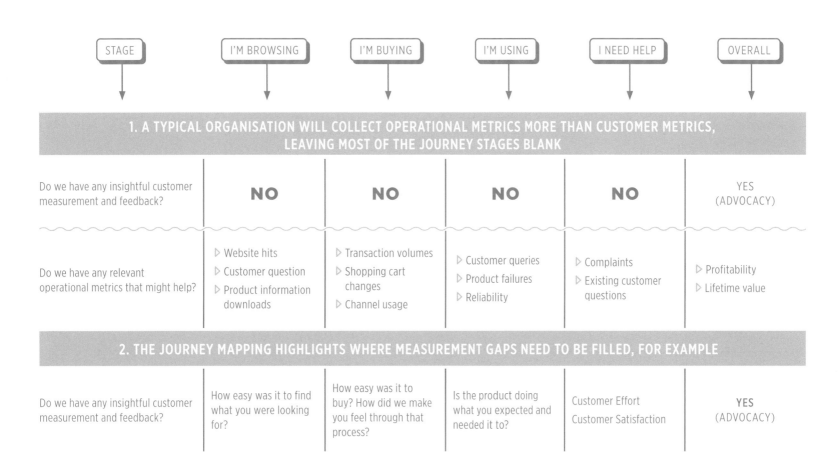

STAGE	I'M BROWSING	I'M BUYING	I'M USING	I NEED HELP	OVERALL
1. A TYPICAL ORGANISATION WILL COLLECT OPERATIONAL METRICS MORE THAN CUSTOMER METRICS, LEAVING MOST OF THE JOURNEY STAGES BLANK					
Do we have any insightful customer measurement and feedback?	**NO**	**NO**	**NO**	**NO**	YES (ADVOCACY)
Do we have any relevant operational metrics that might help?	▷ Website hits ▷ Customer question ▷ Product information downloads	▷ Transaction volumes ▷ Shopping cart changes ▷ Channel usage	▷ Customer queries ▷ Product failures ▷ Reliability	▷ Complaints ▷ Existing customer questions	▷ Profitability ▷ Lifetime value
2. THE JOURNEY MAPPING HIGHLIGHTS WHERE MEASUREMENT GAPS NEED TO BE FILLED, FOR EXAMPLE					
Do we have any insightful customer measurement and feedback?	How easy was it to find what you were looking for?	How easy was it to buy? How did we make you feel through that process?	Is the product doing what you expected and needed it to?	Customer Effort Customer Satisfaction	**YES** (ADVOCACY)

TABLE 4

Using the stages we mapped in the journey mapping workshops to check we are measuring at every stage and for each persona

Refocus stakeholder attention

A good friend started work at a well-known online clothes retailer. The customer satisfaction scores were sky high, well into the 90% to 95% range.

Despite the corporate backslapping and self-congratulation, however, the scores seemed suspiciously high. The company was getting too many complaints for it to be outperforming Customer Experience leaders like Apple, Disney and Amazon. CX professionals need to depend on their instinct; if it feels too good to be true it often is.

It turned out the survey responses were, indeed, scoring very highly. But on closer inspection, it turned out the only customers being asked for feedback were those who received their items but had not complained or returned anything. In short, they were just asking the customers who would be satisfied and, hey presto, the scores were astronomical.

Having carried out several journey mapping workshops, it was clear the survey was being extremely economical with the truth. Using the journey stages identified in the workshops and after much stakeholder management, the survey was extended. It now asked

customers at all four key stages of the journey – I'm browsing, I'm buying, I'm receiving and I need help. What it revealed was a very different picture.

First, it told a clear story of how, of the 100% of customers who started the journey, only around 24% of them reached the final point of having an item delivered (in the right-hand graph on the next page this is shown as the dotted line). They dropped out for a variety of reasons, but it meant the previous survey, as good as the scores were, was only representative of a quarter of their customer base.

Secondly, the scores varied throughout the journey. The "I'm browsing" stage was marked down because would-be customers were unable to navigate their way around the website. Popular items quickly ran out of stock and descriptions of garments were more like over-embellished estate agents' blurb than exciting-but-helpful.

Not surprisingly, the stage of the journey where customers paid their money was quick and easy; management had got that piece sorted out. Deliveries were reliable too, but things fell down again when customers needed help.

All in all, the satisfaction figure percentage plummeted to the mid-60s. That's still not a bad score in

TIP

All metrics must be handled with care and their nuances fully appreciated. If not, everyone chases a score and leaves the experience to chance.

FIGURE 5
Measure the right thing at the right time

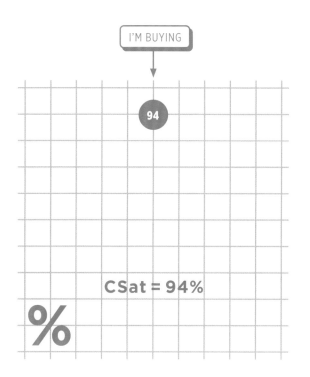

A. Customer satisfaction (CSat)
only measured at the end

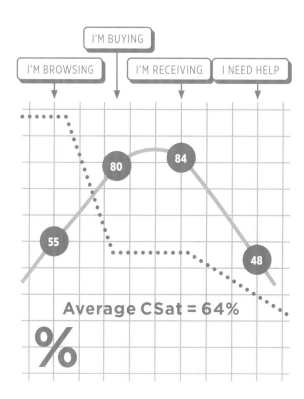

B. When they aggregated the scores for
everyone across each stage ...

itself. However, by putting things in the context of the stages created by the journey mapping it refocused stakeholder attention to where it was needed most. It exposed a culture that was more interested in chasing a number than understanding the experience and – crucially – it made a watertight case for keeping a focus on Customer Experience.

Fill in the gaps

The customer journey for buying a house has never been the quickest of transactions at the best of times. Add in rigorous regulatory requirements and a dependence on a fickle and often slow-moving housing market and the gestation period from enquiry to moving in can be measured in months, if not over a year in some cases. It's fraught with detail. Conversations here, more information there. Not surprisingly it's often a drawn-out emotional rollercoaster.

For one of the UK's largest mortgage lenders, mapping these customer journeys threw a spotlight on just how ineffective their advocacy-based surveys were. Like the fashion retailer example, they were asking for customer feedback only after the mortgage had been set up and

the first payment had been paid. That could be several weeks after the start of the mortgage and many months since the initial application.

The lender shouldn't have been surprised that customers' memories of what it was like were a little hazy. Filling in the gaps highlighted by journey mapping and using additional metrics such as customer effort and satisfaction helped the bank to understand the drivers of advocacy better, to address specific pain-points and make improvements.

TIP
Get the experience right first and the numbers will follow.

In the "What do we measure?" section of your journey mapping workshops it is often only the final stage that has any meaningful customer metrics in it, such as satisfaction or advocacy → (NET PROMOTER SCORE©). If you have stages of the journey where you simply have no measurements, explore how you might fill those gaps.

Satisfaction and effort scores are brilliant indicators to highlight where things are going well or where issues need addressing. Of course, besides the score we need to ask "Why?", which will give us the drivers, the reasons why the scores are what they are.

Asking questions about advocacy is usually done at the end of an experience. Handle it with care though – a customer might have had a brilliant experience in-store but they might have just read some bad press about you. Or, they may not be the sort of person to recommend anything to anyone. In metric-focused cultures, low scores can lead to behaviours that destroy any customer goodwill – gaming the system by telling a customer, "If it's a nine or ten, fill in this survey, if it's eight or below come and talk to me". Hey presto! The reported scores look fantastic but the underlying rot just continues to eat away.

→ NET PROMOTER SCORE

An indicator of how likely a customer is to recommend the company, based on their experience, to a friend or family member.

HOW LIKELY ARE YOU TO RECOMMEND?

Understand and measure how you are making your customers feel; it determines what they say and do next

TIP

Keep your work alive, share it and ask colleagues to critique it.

Customer measurement paves the way for some powerful messaging. If you capture the right measure and overlay your customer data, you're in a strong position to declare that "if a customer is a promoter they are 18 times more likely to come back, spend more and tell everyone they know than a detractor". Or, "every percentage point move on customer satisfaction is worth £1 million to our bottom line – positive or negative".

Your journey mapping has just added heaps more value. You will steer metric-obsessed stakeholders away from focusing on the number to instead looking at what's driving the number. You'll show how more than one customer metric and measuring throughout the journey is essential if you are to build a lasting and effective Customer Experience programme.

6 — SHARE IT WITH COLLEAGUES

In seeking deeper validation earlier, you reached out to colleagues across the business. Their input at that point in time was invaluable, it is now and it will be in future.

Therefore we can keep up the profile of your work and their engagement in it by sharing the journeys on more of an ongoing basis. To avoid the message being too diluted or confusing, choose one journey or a specific customer issue you're focusing on. There are a number of ways to share it and ask for feedback.

Uploading it to an intranet or collaboration platform can reach a wide audience but takes effort on the part of the employee. They need to find time to access it when it suits them, with the obvious risk that they never quite manage to make it a priority.

A lower-tech option might be more appropriate depending on your organisation, how it's structured and its culture. Some of the most effective ways to engage colleagues are the simplest. Here are a few ideas I've seen used across a variety of organisations. Some use just one method, others several.

TO DO LIST

Have the key points of the journey drawn up on a large piece of paper for you to place on a wall. Ideally it would be next to the internal café, kitchen or another high footfall spot. Invite colleagues to take a look and let you know what they think. They can either send you a message or, if you leave a supply of pencils and sticky notes nearby, they can add their thoughts as they are passing.

TABLE TENTS

This is a brilliantly low-cost way of reaching your colleagues. Print one or two key messages or questions arising from your journey mapping (such as "How might we improve our customers' experiences when they renew their contract with us?") on an A4 sheet. If it's mounted on a card structure and can stand alone, drop one onto every desk, put one in every meeting room and on every restaurant table. The remaining A4 sheets can be put on noticeboards around the building; I've even found them on the back of washroom doors.

CUSTOMER CORNER

Find a space in the office where you can, literally, create a customer corner. On a desk, provide a copy of the customer journey you've mapped for colleagues to make their way through. Add copies of the persona profiles and quote relevant verbatim accounts from customer feedback. If it's possible, provide a means by which anyone passing can also listen in to calls or try out the website for themselves.

And again, invite people to provide you with their comments. I once had a flipchart in the middle of an office floor and invited people to jot down their ideas about how to improve the customer journey. It generated many valuable observations but several of them, rather than being handwritten on sticky notes, were printed out. It was mystifying until someone pointed out that the culture was so toxic, employees wanted to speak out about why things were happening but didn't want their handwriting to be recognised for fear of recrimination. Staggering, but an invaluable insight as a by-product of the journey mapping.

TIP

Having done all the hard work, please don't let your journey maps become "expensive dust gatherers".

DON'T WASTE THE JOURNEY

A North American utility company asked me to run journey mapping sessions with their UK arm. In setting up the sessions one of the colleagues recalled they'd done some journey mapping a couple of years previously. Surprisingly (or not, as it turned out) this was news to many on the team. Nonetheless she kindly offered to find it and bring it to the workshops to see what we could carry over and how customer expectations and the company's processes had changed.

Inevitably, the day of the first workshop came and went with no sign of the old journey map. We ploughed on regardless. Word spread around the building about what we were doing and the search for the missing map.

It did turn up, hidden in plain sight. On the floor of the open-plan office of this head office was a row of desk-height stationery cupboards and lockers. On top of them was an array of boxes, printers, spare paper, guillotines and a recent delivery of promotional balloons.

Sandwiched in between and cowering under a sheet of protective glass was our missing journey map. It was ten metres long, a beautifully illustrated visualisation of the paths their customers travel when they move house or switch from a different supplier. Everyone we spoke to said it had been there since they could remember. There was no record of the journey detail anywhere either. It had become, in the words of my good friend and CX globetrotter Ian Golding, a very expensive dust gatherer. All that effort, literally shelved.

Some organisations who are further down the track in terms of their CX maturity will go further still. They create customer rooms, Customer Experience centres or "labs", dedicated spaces which replicate their customers' offices or homes. One of the functions of these rooms is to present an immersive environment in which to map or review customer journeys. It adds a dose of reality, helping colleagues to get inside their customers' heads and "walk in their shoes".

However you do it, sharing your work visually and widely increases the collective ownership and grows your band of informal CX champions right across the business. It keeps your work alive and current as processes, products and services change. It also reduces the chances of a stakeholder catching you out because you weren't aware of key changes; quite the opposite – they'll be impressed at your cross-functional knowledge.

7 — FUTURE-STATE AND DESIGN THINKING

The journeys you've mapped thus far have been all about the "current state"; what is the reality of your customers' experiences, today? You've created a solid starting point from which things can only get better.

If we know where we are starting from, we can find incremental improvements that get rid of wasted effort, remove the sources of frustration. When, and only when, the basics are sorted can we move into the innovative phase of improvement.

It's an absolutely essential foundation block of your Customer Experience programme. By definition however, a "current state" view of the world will lead to fixing things that are broken and improving on what you have today. At some point, we need to break out of that and rethink things completely.

Jeanne Bliss, a genuine "been-there-done-it" thought leader in the world of Customer Experience, draws on a great analogy with an old fairground game when she talks about how organisations miss big opportunities because they are simply content to "whack a mole".

TIP
Having understood how to improve incrementally on where we are today our attention will turn to how we might completely reshape and reinvent the experience, built around the customer, not our legacy processes.

The good news is that the journey mapping methodology we've been through is easily adapted to the "future state". It will run as its own piece of work and requires a more creative mindset, but the core principles are the same and it helps shape your innovative and differentiated experiences of the future.

Your Customer Experience Vision articulates how you want your customers to feel as a result of doing business with you. Your job now is to help design the intentional "perfect" experiences that will create the right emotional response every time.

Your journey framework would therefore take the same steps but the questions would be slightly reframed, as shown in ›Table 5.

TIP
If you use the same journey mapping framework in your "future state" workshops, try starting with customers' emotions. Your CX strategy and vision will guide you, but begin with the question, "How do you want your customers to feel?" In your new, ideal world there will of course be plenty of excitement and positivity with no negative feelings or ambivalence.

TABLE 5
The journey map reframed

STAGES	What will the new stages be? How will they differ from the current state? (Ideally, there will be fewer stages.) Has customers' language changed?
DOING	What will the customer be doing? (Ideally, they will be doing very little to achieve their goals.)
THINKING	What will the customer be thinking? (Any ambiguity or questions are removed. All they think is how reliable, easy, quick and friendly it was.)
FEELING	The key part — what are they now thinking? What emotions will they be sharing with others?
OUR VIEWS	What needs to happen behind the scenes to make this a reality?
MEASURE-MENT	What customer measurement will give us the most insightful facts about this new experience?

Ethnography

Your existing and future customer journeys will be strengthened with further insights you glean by simply observing your customers. Reading their body language, picking up on their non-verbal cues and seeing what they actually do, as opposed to what they say they do, is invaluable.

If you have physical premises your customers come to, take a vantage point and just watch what they do and how they behave. Similarly, visit them or invite them to your office to see how they interact digitally. You'll see the shoulders droop and the eyes roll when things don't go well. You'll see the spring in their step or a satisfied "Yup" when it works.

Don't be afraid to talk to them either. It sounds crazy but so many times I see employees standing right next to a customer but think they're not allowed to talk to them. On occasions, they're unfortunately correct; as one person told me, "I've got to have permission from the Marketing team to chat to a customer".

These opportunities are all direct windows on the lives of your customers. Of course, stay compliant with any data protection laws and be careful not to be seen as a creepy stalker, but you will not regret observing customers at first hand.

Design Thinking

In looking at how you might innovate and rewrite how you do things, you can do a lot worse that taking a Design Thinking approach to your customer experiences. It's quicker than a drawn-out business case methodology but does rely on a culture that is prepared to make mistakes, learn from them, adapt and move on.

As with ethnography, there are many books written on the subject, so I won't labour the point here. It is, however, a great technique to step back from what you know, get into a creative mindset, and explore new and differentiating ideas.

The process, as defined by the *Design Council*, is built around four stages – Discover, Define, Develop and Deliver (›see Figure 6, overleaf.)

TIP

Deconstruct their experience, see first-hand what they actually do, not what they say they will do. Witness the body language and non-verbal clues.

www.designcouncil. org.uk

FIGURE 6
Taking a Design Thinking approach

Discover

insights that highlight particular pain-points or challenges. These might be from your own workshops, customer feedback analysis, complaints investigations or operational metrics.

Define

the customer's problem that needs to be solved. This is a key step as it keeps all the thinking focused. The Design Council has a challenge statement template to help this part of the process: "Given (the problem), how might we help (our persona) do (their functional objective) in a way that makes them feel (something)."

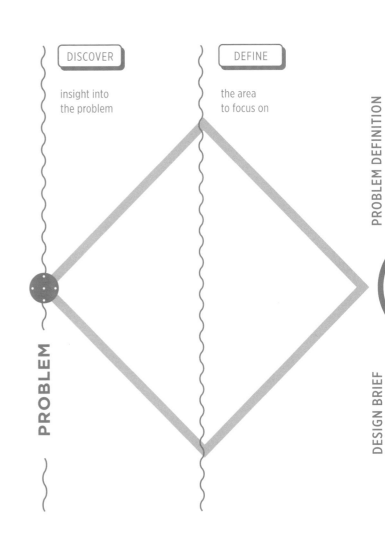

DISCOVER

insight into the problem

DEFINE

the area to focus on

PROBLEM DEFINITION

PROBLEM

DESIGN BRIEF

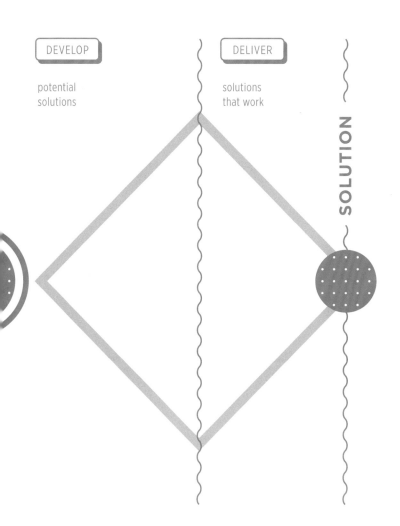

DEVELOP

potential
solutions

DELIVER

solutions
that work

SOLUTION

Develop

a raft of potential solutions and a prototype.
Here's where you and your team get creative
about how your journey might be mapped
in future. Everyone should be sure to avoid
saying, "Yes, but …". Forget today's issues and
processes and get them to say, "Yes, and …".
What would customers least expect you to do?
What can you borrow from other sectors?

Deliver

the right solution. Having tested your prototype, get it to market quickly. It doesn't have
to be 100 % perfect. What does count is the
ability to generate feedback, update your
product or service and deploy any necessary
changes. And so it goes on.

8 — OTHER JOURNEYS TO MAP

Journey mapping is not a one-off exercise. Far from it. To be effective in the long term it has to be an ongoing programme which doesn't – and shouldn't – end.

Now that you have the first journey mapping under your belt, what next?

Plan to remap what you've done

Make a note to revisit the journey map in 12 months, sometimes sooner depending on how quickly your business and market evolves. Your own processes change, competitors up the ante, an IT system upgrade always seems to have an unintended consequence somewhere down the line, and consumer expectations are rising relentlessly. As a result, your mapped journeys can quickly become outdated.

Same persona, different journey

The personas you've looked at will have different experiences with you at different times and in different ways. It might be another product, a different channel (or combination of channels) but you don't want one bad experience to undo all the benefits of a good one. If the original map looked at the overall journey it's likely that there will be smaller journeys within it to unpack. They might not last as long but there are still key pain-points.

For example, in an end-to-end airline journey the "Doing" stages included booking the Executive Lounge at the airport and bags being lost. These micro-journeys can now be the sole focus of a follow-up workshop.

Other personas

It's likely you have several personas you weren't able to include in the original workshop, so make a plan for them. They might all have different needs, products and journeys. And time spent mapping what it's like for a colleague and/or third party to deliver the experience is as invaluable as it is necessary to complete the picture.

Help improve the experience of being an employee; they'll be bigger advocates, they'll go out of their way and they'll want to support your CX movement

9 — MAP EMPLOYEES' EXPERIENCE

Fewer than half of employees would recommend their employer to a friend, according to research by *Glassdoor*[1]. Would you? Have you? *Allegis*[2] found that 69% would not take a job with a company if they had a bad reputation – even if they were unemployed!

There are real commercial benefits of better employee experiences too; Temkin Group helped quantify those in 2016 in a *research study*[3] that looked at the difference between genuinely engaged and disengaged employees:

- *87% of engaged employees will recommend your products and services to someone who might need them, versus 21% of disengaged employees.*

- *82% of engaged employees would do something good for the company even if it was not expected, versus 19% of disengaged employees.*

- *60% of engaged employees will make a recommendation about an improvement, versus 15% of disengaged employees.*

1 GLASSDOOR

"50 HR and Recruiting Statistics for 2016", Glassdoor, May 2016, p. 8.

2 ALLEGIS

Annual Corporate Reputation Survey, CR Magazine and Allegis Group Services, October 2013.

3 RESEARCH STUDY

Temkin Group, 2016, https://experiencematters.blog/wp-content/uploads/2016/08/1609_employee-engagement-infographic.pdf.

The employee journey has many parallels with the customer journey and tolerance of a poor experience is lower. Businesses need to know that their reputation is now shared more widely than ever before.

So if you're looking to create an "employer brand", one where top talent shouts "I want to work for them!", there is good news and bad news. The good news is that whether it's intentional or not, if you have employees you already have an employer experience and therefore an employer brand. The bad news is it may not be the one you want.

The first step is to know what that is today, be clear about what you want it to be in future and get creative about closing any gaps.

This must be done in the context of your company's purpose. Why do you do what you do (beyond making money), what do you do that no other brand does, what makes you excited about working there?

Thankfully, journey mapping can help define what a "great place to work" looks like.

I see many organisations map their customers' journey successfully and reap the benefits of doing so. Far fewer, however, apply the methodology to their people, resulting in a missed opportunity.

The perception of your brand, and of your employees' engagement with it, will vary depending on what stage they are at. A graduate looking across the sector for reasons to work for you will see things differently to a new hire going through the recruitment process, an employee who's been in their job for ten years or a high-level employee who's just been promoted to a director's role.

Understanding the importance of employee engagement is one thing but knowing how to go about it is another. This is why journey mapping is effective: it helps to create empathy and understand how they might be feeling, the challenges they face, or how they will change depending on the individual and how big the gap is.

The methodology for mapping an employee's journey broadly follows the same structure as mapping customers' experiences:

Define the journey

Be very clear about the journey they're on. You may have a particular experience in mind such as the recruitment process, the first 30 days or going through a restructure. To help you find that starting point, you may want to map all of the events across the entire journey from brand awareness, performance reviews and "a typical day" to promotion, exit and retirement. Then you can choose which one(s) you want to drill down into to become a journey or journeys in their own right.

Who are they?

From whose perspective do you want to map the experience? Employee personas will be much the same as for consumers – who are they, what are their goals for that journey and why, what are their pain-points?

TIP
The recruitment process and the first day/week are hugely stressful times – mapping those journeys from the employee perspective will help get their career with you off to a great start.

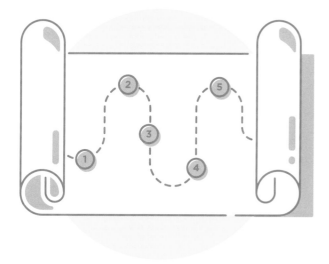

Give the employee journey as much focus as the customer journey

Map the journey

Set out the stages, and for each one look at what they do, think and feel. What do they hope for, wish you would do, or provide? Are they motivated more by flexibility and support than money? How can work fit around their lives better? Capture the internal issues you have as a business that help or get in the way.

Metrics

What data or information do you have access to that shows how well you're doing the important things? What can the employee engagement survey tell you or what do you think is missing from it?

Validate

Sense-check the journey and conclusions with other employees and overlay other relevant feedback you've captured elsewhere.

Do something

Agree the priority areas that need focus and who's going to do it, then keep people updated on progress.

A very simple way to prioritise the issues raised in your employee journey mapping is to compare the things that employees view as important versus how well you do them (› see Figure 7).

TIP

Employee experience surveys are not about whether one-to-ones with your manager happen on time; it's more about, simply, "What's it like to work here and why?"

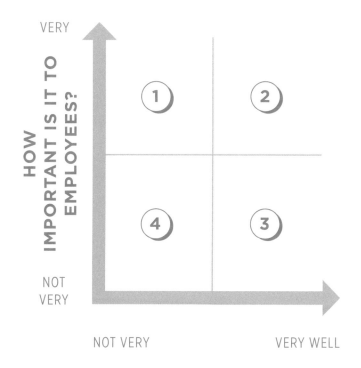

VERY

HOW IMPORTANT IS IT TO EMPLOYEES?

① ②

④ ③

NOT VERY

NOT VERY   VERY WELL

HOW WELL DO WE DO IT?

FIGURE 7
Employee experience

○ *The key area is top left (1) – if there are things your people say are significant but you're not meeting their expectations, focus your efforts here.*

○ *If you have an issue in the top right quadrant (2), where it's important to employees and you do it well, make sure you protect it and share the stories.*

○ *If there's an issue bottom right (3), where you do things well but employees don't much care for it, either explain where the value is (such as performance management reviews) or why it must be done that way.*

○ *For the bottom left (4), where it's not important and not done well, ask why you do it at all. If it needs to be done then explore how you can at least do it well.*

During the mapping activity, your line of questioning should be aimed at identifying what employees care about most. These are good discussion topics for team meetings too. For example:

TIP
A quick way to find out how engaged your employees are – how many of them have 'liked' your Facebook page ...?

▷ Does the leadership team walk the walk when it comes to focusing on customers?

▷ Does everyone know what the vision is for how we want customers to feel?

▷ What makes you distinctive as an employer and how are you communicating that message?

▷ What are your employees saying in terms of what you're getting right? What do they find most frustrating?

▷ What would employees never say (positive or negative)?

▷ How many of your employees engage with your social media activity, have "liked" your Facebook page or follow your LinkedIn page?

▷ If employees were given a branded T-shirt or jacket to wear in town at the weekend, would they be proud enough to do so?

THE CULTURE ON THE INSIDE IS REFLECTED IN THE EXPERIENCE ON THE OUTSIDE. EVERY BUSINESS SHOULD FOCUS AT LEAST AS MUCH ON ITS EMPLOYEES' EXPERIENCES AS IT DOES ON ITS CUSTOMERS' EXPERIENCES – IF NOT MORE.

Addressing employees' issues in this way will show up, not just next time you map the journeys but also in the increase in employee pride and productivity and the decrease in employee turnover and loss of top talent.

CREATE THE NECESSARY GOVERNANCE

Nobody wants more meetings and committees but some I'd argue (of course) are more important than others.

By its nature, Customer Experience must reach up, down, right across and sometimes outside the organisation. To say it must be a harmonious, cross-functional effort is a huge understatement. Your journey mapping has shown the organisation what it must do differently and the reasons why. There now needs to be robust oversight to make sure things do happen.

You may decide that an informal route is best, having regular catch-ups with a group of your CX champions to decide what to do next and who'll do it. At the other extreme you will have a standing agenda slot at the Board and Executive meetings. The senior leadership team will all play a role and while they might lead the strategic-level forum, with your input, you might chair things at a more operational level.

Whatever type of governance it is, you must have a clear mandate of what you are – and are not – responsible for. Widen your net as far as it will go in recruiting colleagues from all parts of the business. Take your journey mapping, customer feedback and other data sources as your input. As a group, you then decide what you'll do, what you need to make that happen, and who's on the hook for delivering it.

You'll bring it all to life for everyone else in the organisation through exciting communications. You'll accept and explain that you can't do everything at once. Prioritising what to do next is no mean feat. You should have no shortage of possible actions, but the mapping exercises will give you a massive hint about what to do first. You will have identified what's most important and how well it's done and that then gives you confidence about what to do in the short, medium and long term for customers, colleagues and stakeholders.

Picking off those things that are easy to implement and have a big impact will also demonstrate the proof of concept for when you are seeking greater investments in time, people and money. What's more, it strengthens your very Customer Experience programme in many ways:

TIP
We can't do this on our own. We must engage top-down and across all functions, whether they are customer-facing or not.

▷ You know how effective your current messaging is about the overall vision and therefore what needs to be done about it. Revisiting your Customer Experience strategy and being absolutely clear about how you want to treat customers has little downside.

▷ You have a genuine peek into what the real culture is and how strong employee engagement is. They may well match the rhetoric but the commitment may also fall short.

▷ You will know what to measure, when and how, and you'll have good arguments for changing the current system.

▷ You have amassed a raft of stories in a very short time. They are invaluable in helping everyone, from the cleaner to the CEO, understand why this approach is so important.

▷ You have rich insights into what the experiences of the future should be if your organisation is going to deliver on its promise.

▷ You have created a buzz about the place. Everyone is talking about how eye-opening your sessions are. The CEO wants you to present at next week's Executive team meeting and colleagues right across the business are getting behind you.

TIP
Journey mapping is all about influencing what should change, what should stop and what should be celebrated.

In terms of specific actions to improve *the* Customer Experience, your governance teases out the most important things and brings them to the surface, using what your journey mapping is telling you and your CX vision and strategy as the guiding principle. If someone asks why you should map a customer journey, it's all about being able to influence people to do one of four things – what should you stop doing, what should you start, what can be improved upon and what should simply carry on as it is today?

Stop

Stop doing things that customers don't value nor is of any value to the business. These are likely to be the sort of experiences that "just happen because we've always done it that way".

Your journey mapping will show the pain-points, the niggles and frustrations customers have day in, day out that you need to remove. They might be known-but-tolerated hinderances or they may be less obvious things that might only become apparent through ethnographic studies. For example, how the shoulders droop and a customer sighs in defeat at the unnecessary need to repeat information. Or, the bad impression created when cleaning equipment is left out in full view because the store cupboard made way for a vending machine.

Start

Introduce new elements, processes, communications and experiences that help your customer succeed in their own goals. Find different ways to make things even easier for them and to evoke the right emotions.

Journey mapping sessions can end with hundreds of ideas, some tactical, some strategic and some cultural. It's simply not practical to do them all, so we need to prioritise. Trying to do too much too soon in an organisation can frighten everyone off. That strategy will appear to lack focus and you can very quickly undo all the good you've created.

Your CX vision and strategy will give you a reference point to help you prioritise. Ritz Carlton famously talk about being "ladies and gentlemen serving ladies and gentlemen." If the idea is adding to that principle, it can be on the priority list of actions.

TIP
Be patient. Be ambitious and push things forward but changing organisational cultures can take years of perseverance.

KEEP THE ACTIONS IN THE CONTEXT OF YOUR COMMERCIAL PRIORITIES; WHAT WILL HELP CUT COSTS, REDUCE CHURN RATES, INCREASE REVENUE AND MARGINS?

Pizza Hut's approach to getting ideas from concept to reality involves three stage-gate questions. The first is: "Is this something the customer has asked for or needs?" The next is: "Will this help at least one customer buy at least one more product?" The last question is: "Will this create a return on investment of at least $1 or 1%?" It's a great philosophy to grow the business organically rather than demanding, as some corporates do, that nothing gets looked at unless it pays for itself in 6 months and has a 40% return in 12 months.

A more traditional model of prioritising is to plot the ideas into a 2x2 matrix. On the vertical axis would be something like "How valuable is this to our customers?", scaled from "Not at all" to "Very" (›see Figure 8).

TIP
Focus on the things that drive the strongest emotions in your customers as they in turn dictate future behaviours.

FIGURE 8
Traditional model of prioritisation

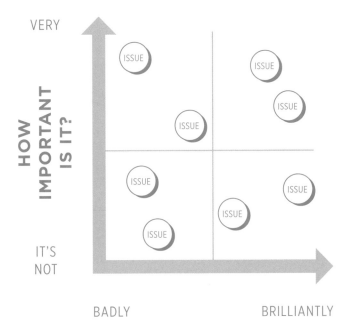

On the horizontal axis might be your control questions. You choose which one to use but you repeat the exercise with more than one question, and you may have others more relevant to you. But, for example, the questions might be:

▷ How valuable is it to our organisation
  (for example, in revenue, margins and brand reputation)?
▷ How easy is it to do
  (for example, time, effort, cost, resources)?
▷ How well does it support our brand proposition?

The relative positioning of your ideas will help move some above others. The ones you recommend for focus will not be "just because" they're good for customers but because you can demonstrate you've given thought to how feasible, economic and strategic they are. You can juggle ideas in the same way that air traffic controllers have a constantly shifting list of aircraft they are guiding – as soon as one lands the next one can be added to the list.

Improve

There are a lot of parallels here with what you may start doing, but this perspective focuses on building on what you already have rather than creating something new.

Of course, we all hope that our journey mapping might change the world and transform customer experiences forever. We like to think that in deconstructing the way customers interact with us and in understanding their motivations we can be the next big disrupter. Future MBA courses will, surely, talk about us in the same sentence as Uber, Airbnb and Netflix.

Until then, the reality is that current state journey mapping will create something equally valuable, if not as headline grabbing. One of the core purposes of this exercise is to create incremental improvements in experiences, to keep demonstrating to customers and employees that you're moving in the right direction. That's the brilliance of this way of mapping because it is so forensic in its analysis of the journey.

The improvements will come in all shapes and sizes at a tactical, strategic and cultural level. You'll find there are many quick wins to be had. It might be a subtle

TIP
We won't all be the next Disney, Amazon, Moo or Netflix. But taking a genuine customer focus means we can at least be more like them than our competitors are.

process change, moving in-store furniture around, an update to the website to avoid ambiguity or a pilot to gauge the impact of a particular upgraded experience.

Some improvements will be more strategic and medium term in nature. These will need more thought, planning and cross-functional collaboration. For an airport, it might be making improvements to their signage through the terminal. For a SaaS company (Software as a Service) it might be finding ways to bring the Customer Success and product development teams closer together. Or for a dental practice, it might be moving from a "We're the experts" brand proposition to "Be more relaxed and confident".

Journey mapping may also highlight the need for changes at a cultural level. The conversations you've had or overheard may point to a lack of perceived commitment by the leadership team. It may not be clear what the overall vision is and how everyone can play their part. And until the culture is perfectly in tune with its customers, it may be that there is simply no meaningful reward or recognition for employees to help customers.

TIP

In the day-to-day activity it's easy for organisations to create poor experiences unintentionally. How quickly they pick up on that and how they respond is a real window into their true culture.

Carry on

Journey mapping by its nature tends to focus on fixing broken processes and making improvements to things that are not great. The tone can sometimes feel like it's all a little bit negative.

However, your work should necessarily also highlight the good things you are doing today and protect them. You'll hear some fantastic stories of generosity and kindness on the part of colleagues towards customers. Where they embody everything your brand stands for, it's key to capture and share those anecdotes, showing great examples of the behaviours and attitudes everyone is looking for.

It clearly illustrates the absolute requirement to not lose what's made you successful and customer-centric so far. As businesses grow, become part of other companies or go through an "organisational transformation" (often, only to be a very similar version of their previous selves) it's easy to lose the good stuff, unintended or not.

DON'T LOSE CUSTOMER-CENTRICITY

John Lewis, one of the UK's favourite department store retailers, has lived to tell its own cautionary tale in recent years.

For decades it was a darling of the high street, a go-to choice for many discerning shoppers. Instore, the level of attention to customer service was the envy of many businesses around the world.

Their employees are partners in the business, meaning they have a vested interest in helping to make sure customers come back, buy more of the higher-margin products and tell their family and friends to do the same.

The formula worked superbly, with employees enjoying regular pay rises and bonuses that other shop workers could only dream of.

But while the instore experience was setting the bar by which others were measured, the online delivery service was unravelling itself. While some buyers received what they'd ordered and were perfectly happy, others were having very different experiences.

By the end of 2019 the company's Trustpilot score in the UK was just 2 out of 5 from 10,000 reviews. Customers complained that their questions or complaints were unanswered, that replacement products too were damaged and there was a lack of ownership to resolve any issues. Alongside the "Awesome" and "Still love them" comments is a worrying flow of customers saying, "It's just not what you expect from John Lewis. Never again" and "I've been a customer of theirs for years but will not be using them again".

Covid-19 has simply piled more pressure onto what were already challenging trading conditions for retailers. Even John Lewis' legendary salary bonus was just 2% for 2019/20. As their new CEO steadies the ship, we can but hope that they win back those lost online customers.

The point being, they get things so right instore, yet for some reason that has not always been the case in the online world. An expensive lesson others will do well to avoid.

INFLUENCE

Customer journey mapping will be pointless if nothing happens as a result. For that reason I'm including one last, very relevant section on influence.

To have people want to join your movement, to get them to change their behaviours and agree there's a case for change, you need influence. It may come from your own knowledge, charm and credibility but to many, it seems, customers are still a pain in the proverbial.

It goes to the very core of what makes a Customer Experience professional tick, what makes them so passionate about the subject. You might be fortunate to push on an open door but in case that door is proving sticky, I'd like to share a few thoughts from good friend and global Customer Experience specialist Ian Golding. He talks about three perspectives on how you can increase your influence.

TIP
Journey mapping creates the facts and the evidence about what should change and why.

AWARENESS, INFLUENCE AND ACTION: THREE THINGS YOUR JOURNEY MAPPING WILL CREATE.

Borrowed authority

If you have access to someone in your leadership team who "gets it" and will back you, make the most of that opportunity. Use their influence and strategic leaning to help others realise this is an important, organisation-wide activity. They can help open doors for you, make introductions and break down the internal walls of silos.

That support is invaluable because not everyone will engage easily. With the right approach, even the most political and sceptical of people will think, "If it's important to them then it should be important to me."

Handle with care though. Journey mapping should not be seen as "We've got to do this because the CEO says so." It's about spreading the word that the future of the company for everyone depends on being more customer-centric.

Borrowed authority also wears thin after a while. And in some cases the person you are leaning on changes role. So be prepared.

Positional authority

This can be the trickiest, as it's pretty much based on your job title.

It's unlikely you'd try and win people over by saying, "Look, I'm the Customer Experience Transformation Manager so you have to come to my workshop" but I can assure you that has happened and with predictable consequences.

The organisation hired you and gave you responsibility for Customer Experience. You may have "been there, done that", you may be paid well and have a fantastic job title, but that doesn't mean people will listen.

If it is the only reason why people should follow you, that too will run out of steam.

Earned authority

This "authority" comes in the form of proven credibility. People see what you've done, how you've done it and the impact it has had.

As we mentioned at the start, Steve Covey, author of *The 7 Habits of Highly Successful People*[1] said, "Seek first to understand then be understood." It's so true. Get out and about in your organisation to understand how

1 Covey, S. R., *The 7 Habits of Highly Successful People*, Simon & Schuster, UK, 2004.

it works, how it makes its money, what its challenges are and where customers fit in. If you can, experience what it's like for a customer.

Empathising with your colleagues in a commercial way will get them engaged and interested. And if you have not done a journey mapping session with a large cross-functional group before, you can still create a proof of concept. Gather a few customer-centric colleagues together and talk through a particular customer journey.

You can then go back out to the business and say, "We did XYZ and as a result we have changed this process which reduces costs, wasted effort and makes life much easier for customers." It's a snapshot of what's to come and will make others curious, and sign up to be part of what you're creating.

Of course, you may simply be one of those people who have a gift for influencing, speaking and writing with absolute clarity, charm and infectious enthusiasm. Please let me know how you do it.   «

STAY IN TOUCH

jerryangrave@empathyce.com

CLOSING THOUGHTS

There's no single, absolutely right way to approach it but I hope this *Playbook* gives you a little direction to guide you on your own journey of journey mapping.

Exactly how you go about it, making it part of your wider Customer Experience programme and influencing those who can help you change things is up to you. You know what works best for you, but I trust in some small way the thoughts in this book give you added structure and confidence in what you're doing.

The concept of "Customer Experience" has been at the top of business agendas for many years now, yet it's not something an organisation chooses to do. If there is a customer, by definition they are already having a "customer experience". The principles have been around since humans traded clubs for wheels.

If history teaches us anything it's that customer empathy, the understanding that shapes those customer experiences, will be all the more important as businesses return to a post-Covid-19 world. The needs, wants, fears and expectations of customers may well have changed. The corporate vision may be untouched, so it will be the Customer Experience programme, the strategy and people like you who will be at the centre of the effort.

It's not easy. There will be plenty of hurdles put in your way, but you will find a way over them.

If it feels lonely, remember there is a fantastic and generous community of Customer Experience professionals (www.cxpa.org) out there, ready to offer words of advice and encouragement should you need it.

If you feel like you're the only one who gets it, ask your sceptical stakeholders what they did after their last poor experience. Did they go back to that restaurant where the waiter was rude? Did they complete the customer feedback form for the internet service provider they just complained about? The penny will drop, I promise.

If you don't know where to start, if it all feels overwhelming, grab a coffee with a friend, decide on one very clear journey and one familiar persona and map their journey in your notebook.

If I can leave you with one message about customer journey mapping, I'll repeat what I said earlier: if you do nothing else in the name of Customer Experience give journey mapping a go and see where it takes you.

I sincerely hope the notes in this book prove useful. Do stay in touch, I'd love to hear your own customer journey mapping stories.

Happy mapping!

JERRY ANGRAVE

ACKNOWLEDGE-MENTS

I 'm eternally grateful to Karen Hoar and Jayne Hall whose infectious enthusiasm for Customer Experience had a material impact on me and still does to this day.

I've made many lasting friendships by being a very small part of a large and sharing global community of Customer Experience professionals. To them all, thank you. I'm so pleased that Ian Golding penned the Foreword. His knowledge and passion for the subject is legendary. He's taught me a huge amount but beyond that he's a good mate, the sort of caring and reliable friend we all need.

Thank you too, Steve Hardman, as publisher, for your guidance, endless patience and friendship.

And lastly but not unexpectedly, thank you Caroline, Charlie and Freya. You may not be overly interested in the subject matter of the book itself but to be on the receiving end of your unconditional love and support is something for which I am truly grateful.

ABOUT THE AUTHOR

JERRY
ANGRAVE

Jerry Angrave is Customer and Passenger Experience Director at Empathyce, a customer experience (CX) consulting and coaching company.

Jerry works across many sectors including aviation and travel, financial services, professional services and manufacturing. Based in the United Kingdom, he works with companies throughout Europe and the Middle East.

His work is about helping build stronger CX programmes through the development of effective CX strategies and the delivery of operational competencies. At its core is the understanding of customers; who they are, why they do business and their hopes, expectations and fears.

The value in customer journey mapping is therefore in unlocking the most important issues and prioritising what should be done about them. Jerry has facilitated hundreds of journey mapping workshops and trained countless CX practitioners to run their own sessions.

He is a member of the Customer Experience Professionals Association, created in 2011 to support CX professionals globally. Jerry is hugely passionate about helping those who are looking to build a CX-based career to gain increased knowledge and confidence so they can contribute more to their organisation.

Jerry spent many years in senior CX roles with corporate organisations, including Lloyds Banking Group, before establishing Empathyce in 2012.

ISBN 978-3-11-064111-0
e-ISBN (PDF) 978-3-11-064133-2

Library of Congress Control Number: 2020940475

Bibliographic information published by the Deutsche Nationalbibliothek
The Deutsche Nationalbibliothek lists this publication in the Deutsche
Nationalbibliografie; detailed bibliographic data are available on the internet
at http://dnb.dnb.de.

www.degruyter.com